STUDIES IN AMERICAN LITERATURE

Volume XXVII

☆☆☆☆☆☆☆☆☆☆☆☆☆☆☆☆☆☆☆☆☆☆☆☆☆☆☆☆☆☆☆☆

O. Henry about 1900.

FROM ALAMO PLAZA TO JACK HARRIS'S SALOON

O. Henry and the Southwest He Knew

by

JOSEPH GALLEGLY
Rice University

1970
MOUTON
THE HAGUE · PARIS

LIBRARY OF CONGRESS CATALOG CARD NUMBER: 70-123125

Printed in The Netherlands by Mouton & Co., Printers, The Hague.

To Elizabeth, Richard, Rick, Laura, and John.

PREFACE

I have long believed that a reader could more fully appreciate the humor of O. Henry's stories of the Southwest if he would take time to gain better acquaintance with the people and social conditions of that geographical area during the years about which the author wrote. To William Sydney Porter, Texas and other sections of the Southwest, old and new, were as familiar as the Mississippi river was to Mark Twain, or as the "old" Southwest was to George Washington Harris and Johnson Jones Hooper.

With the conviction that O. Henry reflects the life and times of his region as faithfully as does any other great American humorist, I have prepared the historical and critical study that fills the pages of this little volume. It is my earnest hope that the reader may derive a wholesome benefit from a work that has given me considerable pleasure in the making.

ACKNOWLEDGMENTS

I am indebted to many who have helped me in the preparation of this work. My wife, Carmen Margaret Gallegly, has been of assistance to me in more ways than I can find words to explain; Mrs. W. P. Gaddis, of Cotulla, Texas, an O. Henry specialist in her own right, has furnished both encouragement and substantial help; the late Messrs. Julius Tengg, of San Antonio, and Wilmer Waldo, of Houston, provided me with many worthwhile historical facts; Mr. S. W. Pease, of San Antonio, has obliged me with several interesting bits of San Antonio history; Mrs. Charlena W. Williams, the Rice English Department secretary, has given helpful suggestions as well as material aid.

Officials of both the Southern Pacific and the Missouri Pacific railroads have given substantial aid of appreciable value. I wish to thank also Mr. Ted James of San Antonio for supplying me with a number of illustrations which will noticeably enhance the value of the book. Dr. William S. Dix, librarian of the Princeton University Library, very courteously furnished me with a microfilm of the musical comedy, *Cinderella at School,* an item that I found of value in developing one of my theses.

I am greatly indebted likewise to the American Book Company for permission to allude to several statements in "The Financial Background", of the "Introduction" to the publisher's *Mark Twain* (1935), a book of the American Writers Series, by Fred Lewis Pattee; to Appleton-Century-Crofts for the use of material from Arthur Hobson Quinn, *A History of the American Drama from the Civil War to the Present Day* (1927); to Argosy-Antiquarian, Ltd., for allowing me to make references to passages in *The Trail*

Drivers of Texas (1967); to the Arthur H. Clark Company, for generously permitting me to refer to a chapter in Volume I of *Athanase de Mézières, and the Louisiana Frontier, 1768-1780*, an historical work by Herbert Eugene Bolton (1914); to the Cambridge University Press for letting me quote words from Volume IV of Allardyce Nicoll's *A History of English Drama* (1955); to Columbia University Press for the right to quote a sketch from George C. D. Odell, *Annals of the New York Stage*; to the University of Pennsylvania Press for letting me make reference to a passage from E. Hudson Long, *O. Henry, the Man and His Work* (1949); to Charles Scribner's Sons, for allowing me to quote from George Santayana, *Dominations and Powers* (1951).

I owe an especial debt of gratitude to Doubleday and Company for giving me permission to refer to and quote from the following specifically named stories by O. Henry. All of these stories bear the copyright of this publishing firm under the dates indicated: "Seats of the Haughty", (1906); "The Indian Summer of Dry Valley Johnson", (1907); "The Chair of Philanthromathematics", (1907); "The Hiding of Black Bill", and "The Moment of Victory", (1908); "A Fog in Santone", and "The Friendly Call", (1910); and "A Technical Error", (1910); I am also indebted to Doubleday and Co. for the right to refer to a scene from Arthur W. Page, "Little Pictures of O. Henry", (1928).

Mr. Chris Emmett, of Dallas, author of *Shanghai Pierce, A Fair Likeness*, has kindly allowed me to appropriate an incident from this interesting book of his authorship. I am grateful to Mr. Emmett for this courtesy. I must also acknowledge an obligation to Grosset and Dunlap for the use of a scene from this company's edition of *The Hoosier Schoolmaster,* by Edward Eggleston. The references to Bret Harte's stories are to volumes in the Riverside Edition of *The Writings of Bret Harte,* by the Houghton Mifflin Company. Harper and Row, Incorporated, kindly consented to my making references to and quoting from Mark Twain's "Fenimore Cooper's Literary Offences"; this publisher likewise allowed me to refer to an incident in Frank X. Tolbert, *An Informal History of Texas* (1961). Mr. Tom Lea, author of *The Brave Bulls,* allowed me to refer to the "sentience passage" from his novel of that title. I am also pleased to acknowledge an obligation to the Macmillan Company for references to and quotations from this publisher's edition of *Alice in Wonderland*. In addition, I am grateful to the University of North Carolina Press for the use of material from Virgil Carrington Jones' *The Hatfields and the McCoys* (1948). I am also grateful to the Oxford University Press for facts taken from the *Oxford Companion to English Literature*, as well as from the *Oxford Companion to American Literature*.

To the Princeton University Press I am grateful for being allowed to make several allusions to the plot and characters of Bartley Campbell's "My Partner", and to a scene in Charles H. Hoyt's "A Temperance Town". Both of the dramas mentioned are found in the Princeton Press edition of *America's Lost Plays*, copyright, 1940. For an incident in an adventure of Sherlock Holmes, I am indebted to the John Murray edition of *The Complete Sherlock Holmes Short Stories* (1928).

I must also express my warm thanks to Dr. Joseph A. Ward, Chairman of the English Department, to Dean Virgil W. Topazio, and to President Frank E. Vandiver, all of Rice University, for making it possible for my work to go to press.

I should feel remiss indeed if I neglected to indicate how grateful I am to the hundreds of members of my English 395 classes at Rice for encouraging me to develop and expand my studies of O. Henry. Much of the matter found in this book first took articulate form in my Southwestern and Western life and literature classes at Rice.

In conclusion, I feel urged to say that the cooperation shown by the individuals and publishers listed in this acknowledgment added greatly to the smoothness by which this work was accomplished.

15 March 1970   Joseph S. Gallegly

CONTENTS

14

PROLOGUE

San Antonio in the seventies and eighties of the past century, like Gaul, was divided into three parts: Anglo-Americans, a group that included inhabitants of Irish, Scots and English extraction, as well as settlers themselves from the British Isles; the Germans, natives of various provinces of the Fatherland, together with the sons and daughters of those who had taken up their abode in the Alamo City in the forties; and, lastly, the Mexicans, or Spanish-speaking element, a group that included the descendants of the Canary Island settlers, and their more numerous darker-hued brethren, chiefly of Coahuiltecan Indian blood.[1]

The Anglo-Americans furnished peace-officers, saloon-keepers, robbers of many sorts and kinds (train, bank, cattle, horses and such), gamblers, wool and lawful cattle dealers and growers, bankers, lawyers, clergymen, Rangers, merchants, and representatives of sundry major and minor professions. The German element for the most part supplied the brewers, millers, hardware merchants, lumber dealers, musicians, stationers, bankers, lawyers, architects and builders. The ethnic group denominated by the term Mexican supplied the city with an abundance of artisans, skilled and unskilled (among whom were stone and brick masons), faggot peddlers, water-venders, mocking-bird salesmen, grocers, itinerant confectioners, and proprietors of outdoor cafés. Another ethnic class which I suppose should be mentioned in passing was comprised of blacks and griffes. These people operated gen-

[1] For an accurate account of the Coahuiltecan Indian tribes in Texas see Herbert Eugene Bolton, *Athanase de Mézières and the Louisiana-Texas Frontier, 1768-1780*, I, 62, 63.

erally in a menial capacity, performing functions of a subordinate nature. For a reason that Yankees and some foreigners could never understand many were employed as cooks.

The Anglo-Saxons, of course, spoke variants of the many brogues and dialects based on the English tongue; the Germans for a long while hung tenaciously to the dialects of the provinces of their homeland, but after some years yielded to pressure and adopted the language of their Saxon cousins. This they developed into a fairly satisfactory means of verbal intercourse. They of course spoke the vernacular with a few little twists and overtones, but these peculiarities lent distinction and charm to their speech. The Mexicans showed a reluctance to forsake their versions of the Galician and Andalucian dialects, and to this day make their thoughts known to one another in a corrupt form of Castilian.

A visitor to San Antonio in the eighties would have noticed that a substantial segment of the populace showed an eagerness to attain culture. Historians have led us to believe that a wholesome desire of that sort never disturbed the minds of the provincials of that era; lawlessness, they write, and the outward flourishes of untrammelled and misdirected vigor, blotted out the healthy wishes of such precursors of civilization as the Texans of that period were. There would seem to be some question as to whether the foregoing statement is applicable in all the cases to which it is directed. The San Antonio *Daily Express* reported on July 4, 1882, that Swarthmore College (presumably an institution of learning in the city) had reopened in a new building, with Edward H. Magill as president. From the same issue of this journal we learn that W. C. Rote, superintendent of public instruction in the city, had a staff of learned linguists to instruct pupils in a one-hundred-thousand-dollar stone high school building. Professor Rote must have been making progress of a sort, for a few years earlier, another newspaper of the city declared that the Professor's teachers institute had been barren of results.[2] The paper lamented that Prof. Rote had had "teachers analyzing

[2] *The Surprise*, I, No. 2 (June, 1879).

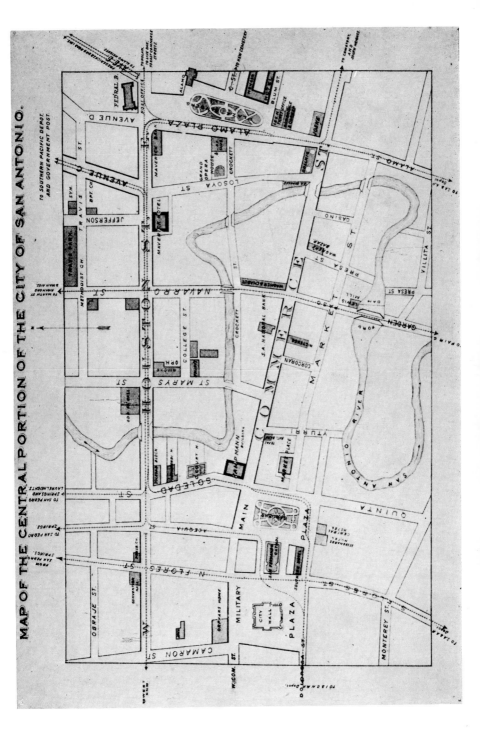

MAP OF THE CENTRAL PORTION OF THE CITY OF SAN ANTONIO.

Milton (a young ladies' boarding school exercise) during the full year, instead of instructing them in practical methods of teaching". A year later the *Evening Light* was to carry the disappointing news of another failure in the realm of education: Professor F. M. Halbedl's Summer Normal had proved unsuccessful.[3] Of the twenty teachers who registered at this session, five (the *Light* said) were from the country, "two were not teachers at all, and if we deduct the Superintendent and his son, only eleven who are of our public schools remain. No shining spectacle." [4]

San Antonio, however, was not utterly barren ground as far as college material was concerned; or at least institutions of learning elsewhere did not think so. An advertisement in the *Daily Express* indicated that those wishing to attend lectures in the University of Virginia law school should apply to John B. Minor, professor of common and statutory law at the university.[5] Dr. R. M. Swearingen somewhat later appealed to the ambitious young ladies of the city. His Alta Vista Institute at Austin (his notice in the paper said) would open its fifteenth annual session on September 4, 1882.[6]

A distressing rumor had circulated in the city in June of 1879. The news got about town that school children would have to pay ten cents a week when the public schools opened their doors again in September. "The blow is aimed at popular education", *The Surprise* deplored.[7] June of that year seemed to be somewhat of a memorable month in the educational world. A group of responsible men of color met to petition Superintendent Rote to have the city "employ negro teachers for negro children". These men of color would seem to have been of the same mind as the philosopher George Santayana when he declared that "the Negro, if he is not a fool, loves his own inspiration, and expands in the society of his own people".[8] *The Surprise* found the action of the blacks hard to understand. Said the journal:

---

3   San Antonio *Evening Light* (July 30, 1883).
4   *Ibid.*
5   San Antonio *Daily Express* (July 2, 1882).
6   *Ibid.* (July 5, 1882).
7   *The Surprise*, I, No. 2 (June, 1882).
8   *Dominations and Powers*, XV, 358.

It is just what their worst enemies would have them do. They have been demanding all along that no distinction be made against them in public institutions and now they demand colored teachers for colored children.[9]

During O. Henry's Texas days, the horse was as important an item of trade as the cow; and in the eighties, San Antonio was the leading horse market in the United States.[10] The horse as a means of travel was as important to man then as the automobile is now; and owners of the quadrupeds were much more touchy about losing favorite mounts than their grandsons are today about losing their "souped-up jalopies". Many a culprit in those days was hanged from an oak or hackberry limb just for having mistaken someone else's horse for his own.

Traders came from far and wide to buy horses at the South Flores street markets in Santone. On September 19, 1882, John Longnecker of Atlanta, Illinois, left the city with eight carloads of mares he had bought on South Flores. "A Texas mare is ambitious and has lots of bottom", the buyer was quoted as having said. He then explained that he planned to cross the mares with the "unambitious" Norman stallions of the north. The average cross-bred animal, Longnecker said, would sell for $150, although he had sold one or two for as high as $800.[11]

During May of 1886, 6885 horses were shipped from the city by rail; the number was 2,555 in excess of those shipped in the previous year for the same month.[12]

San Antonio at this period was of great importance also as a wool market. Ed Buckley was the most prominent wool buyer in Texas, as well as a "large" grower of the commodity. (The name of Buckley appears to have fascinated O. Henry; he has used it in two of his Texas stories.) [13] Buckley bought for Robson Brothers of Philadelphia.[14] In the city, as might be expected of the wool

---

[9]   The Surprise, I, No. 2 (June, 1882).
[10]   J. Frank Dobie, A Vaquero of the Brush Country, XIV, 186.
[11]   San Antonio Evening Light (September 19, 1882).
[12]   The Evening Paper (June 9, 1886).
[13]   See "An Afternoon Miracle", and "Friends in San Rosario", The Complete Works of O. Henry, I, 165, 451.
[14]   There were fifteen other wool-buying firms in the city. Among these were Sam C. Bennett; Berg and Brother; Chabot and Moss; A. J. T. Beaure-

center of the Southwest, Messrs. Claridge and Allen edited and published *The Texas Wool Journal*, a distinctive publication that was greatly respected by members of the trade. The importance of San Antonio as a wool market can be understood better if one cites a few figures illustrative of the extent of the trade in this commodity. In 1882, 7,607,251 pounds of the staple were shipped by rail from the city, 150,000 pounds going to a mill in New Braunfels.[15]

With the development of the railroads and the gradual closing of the trails to the north, San Antonio became a leading cattle market. Former trail-driver and cattleman George W. Saunders was prominently identified with the establishment of a cattle mart in the city. In 1886, Saunders, with Captain John T. Lytle, Jess Presnall, W. H. Jennings and others formed a company and built the Union Stock Yards.[16] Other cattlemen such as Dillard Fant, Col. Ike T. Pryor, and George West, with San Antonio as their headquarters, remained active in cattle trading for years.

In 1889, a typical year, 84,000 head of cattle were bought and sold in the city, as well as two million cowhides. For the same year, 70,000 horses were traded, 160,000 head of sheep and seven million pounds of wool.[17]

A characteristic of the cultural side of the life of the German-American citizens was reflected in the large number of singing associations these people organized and maintained. There were the Teutonia Singing Association, the Beethoven Maennerchor, the Mendelssohn Singing Club, the Turner Maennerchor, and the Orion Singing Club. The Beethoven Maennerchor arranged a notable Saengerfest in April of 1887. Taking part in the festival were grand choruses of male and female voices, four with a full orchestra and two without. The mixed choruses of the city alone comprised one hundred and twenty voices.[18]

gard; Louis Bergstrom; Bergstrom and Mauermann; I. Efrom and Company; A. B. Frank and Co.; Colonel T. C. Frost; M. Halff and Brother; Ed Kotula and Company; Lobatt and Co.; B. Oppenheimer and Company; Oothant and Nash; and Staffel and Vogel (San Antonio *City Directory* of 1883-1884).

15 San Antonio *City Directory* of 1883-1884.
16 *The Trail Drivers of Texas*, I, 449.
17 William Corner, *San Antonio de Bexar*, page 63.
18 *The Evening Paper* (June 5, 1886).

Even at the beergardens one could find high quality entertainment. Ludwig Mahnke's concerts at the Mission Garden were especially notable. On June 4, 1886, Messrs. Slazer and Steinheim, "Vienese duettests", opened a five-day engagement at this establishment. They were assisted by Miss Papi Ramersdorff, "a comely young lady with a strong soprano voice, and a wonderfully facile yodel, which she introduced to great advantage".[19] A few years earlier a program at Mahnke's Garden included these popular numbers: "I Dreamed I Slept in Marble Halls", from *The Bohemian Girl* by Balfe; "My Song", by Gumbert; "The Flower Girl", by Berganni; and "The Waltz Song", by Arditti.[20]

Contributing measurably to a Vienna Singerstrasse-like atmosphere was the free flow of E. Anhueser Company's lager beer.[21] It is very likely that some patrons found locally brewed beer more to their taste. Wilhelm Esser and Charles Degan, both brewers of the city, offered their brew for sale in drinking places throughout the community. Many also may have preferred the lager of W. J. Lemp, another St. Louis brewer.

The Vienna singers were to visit the city off and on for quite a long period. A few years after the appearances recorded at Mahnke's, these entertainers gave a grand concert every night during the week at the Pavilion on Losoya Street back of the Post Office Exchange.[22]

The interested visitor to San Antonio or a citizen of the city could find music every evening and a special concert on Sunday at Muth's Concert Pavilion on Government Hill across from the Army Post. Mr. Muth's "ad" in the papers said that the "choicest brands of wines, liquors, cigars, and fresh cool beer were always on hand and served in royal style". Patrons of Muth's could see the "dress parade by U. S. troops and hear music by a military band on parade-grounds directly opposite the pavilion".[23]

In the matter of health and welfare, the San Antonian (as in-

---

19   *Ibid.* (June 9, 1886).
20   San Antonio *Evening Light* (August 31, 1883).
21   In 1882, four hundred carloads of this Saint Louis brew were sold in San Antonio (Stephen Gould, *Alamo City Guide* of 1882).
22   *The Evening Paper* (June 9, 1886).
23   *The Evening Light* and *Daily Express, passim,* 1887-1888.

deed was the case with the dweller in other U. S. cities of the period) could derive comfort from sundry panaceas and specifics offered at drug stores in the form of bitters and tonics of other sorts. *Hostetter's Bitters* met perhaps with more general acceptance, but *Brown's Iron Bitters* must have made an appeal to many of the ailing. The Reverend G. W. Rice, editor of *The American Christian Review* commended the remedy with the fervor of a zealot. Said Mr. Rice:

The foolish wasting of vital forces in business, pleasure, and vicious indulgence of our people, makes your preparation a necessity; and if applied, will save hundreds who resort to saloons for temporary recuperation.[24]

The makers of *Hostetter's Bitters* advanced no such claims for their product.[25] But the Swift Specific company declared in an advertisement in 1884 that "experience in the treatment of cancer with Swift's Specific would seem to warrant us in saying that it will cure this dreaded scourge".[26]

Actually one might reasonably deduce from claims made for the health-giving properties of Western Texas weather that few of the citizens of San Antonio would ever have need for patent medicines.

"Purest atmosphere, sir, on earth! ... our air contains nothing but ozone, sir, pure ozone", O. Henry declares in one of his stories.[27] William Corner devotes a few pages in *San Antonio de Bexar* to the city as a health resort, especially for consumptives, who undoubtedly found the dry air of the region of much benefit. Corner discounts the dangers of the dreaded "northers", and is supported in his views by a learned physician of the city, Dr. Cupples. The doctor is quoted as giving a sober, factual analysis of the virtues of the city's climate, modestly affirming that the long hot summers could be "wearisome to an invalid", but that the mild winters could be pleasant and helpful.[28]

---

[24] *Daily Express* (July 4, 1882).
[25] *Ibid.* (July 6, 1882).
[26] *Ibid.* (March 5, 1884).
[27] "A Fog in Santone", *The Complete Works of O. Henry*, II, 992.
[28] William Corner, *op. cit.*, pages 58-61.

At the time of O. Henry's arrival in the Nueces country (in 1884), T. N. Smith, M. D., was claiming that the two-year-old town of Cotulla (population 1,200) had a mild climate and health-giving waters with remarkable curative properties. The doctor strongly suggested that persons with frail constitutions spend some time at the south Texas spa and presumably let nature's restorative do for them what Brown's *Bitters* was doing for others.

It was about this time, too, that the Reverend Henry Ward Beecher visited the city to make an appeal to the thoughtful and serious-minded citizens with his lecture, *The Reign of the Common People.* The cultured and curious paid $1.50 a seat on this first day of October, 1883, to hear the eminent divine. The manager of Casino Hall said that he had secured the services of Beecher at great expense.

Baseball, which was to become the great American game, was certainly in its swaddling clouts in San Antonio. This game, declared by some to have been invented by Abner Doubleday and by others to have developed from an earlier game of "rounders", in 1883 was just beginning to attract the attention of the sports-minded in the Alamo City.[29]

The *Evening Light* of July 28, 1883, carried an interesting dispatch about a baseball game played in the city the day before.

Yesterday afternoon the San Antonio Blues met the Olis base ball club, composed of soldiers, at the springs, where, after a fairly good game, they once more proved their superiority by beating their opponents 21 to 6. The fielding of the Olis club was poor, while their catcher and pitcher were not up to average. The Blues showed great improvement, and the more practice they have the better they will be each time.

One gathers from a perusal of this notice that the Olis club boys were not particularly brilliant either in the field or at the plate. It is to be noted also that the game was strictly a contest between teams, a fact that should have pleased the managers; not a single player of either club was called by name.

[29] [Baseball's] resemblance to rounders is merely a coincidence, and it had its origin in the United States, probably at Cooperstown, New York, in 1839, when, it is said, Abner Doubleday devised a scheme for playing it. (Edward Breck, "Base-Ball", *Encyclopedia Britannica*, Eleventh Edition, III, 458.)

The results of another game were recorded in the same issue of the journal. The Lorgnettes (a somewhat whimsical designation for a ball club) beat the Houston Nationals by a score of 20 to 12. The Lorgnettes were of Galveston. The short account closed with the comment: Poor game.

Lawn tennis was another sport that was finding support among the young people of San Antonio. The Zingaree Lawn Tennis club had twelve members; the Endymion, more liberal in its make-up, numbered among its sixteen members eight women and eight men. If Zingaree is a corruption of the Italian word "zingaro", meaning gypsy, and the name, as well as Endymion – a handsome Greek youth – was literally applied, one can deduce that segments of the populace from top to bottom were going in for tennis.

Organizations of a highly moral nature were making appeals to certain of the conscientious among the citizenry. The Friends of Temperance of San Antonio, Lodge No. 530 met "under pleasant surroundings in a flower-bedecked hall". There was a legend set forth on a screen: "Temperance, Fidelity, Truth". This meeting, however, was poorly attended.[30]

A large proportion of the San Antonio populace, it is reasonable to assume, like that of any other city of comparable size in America at that time, derived wholesome pleasure from a day's outing in the country or at a park. The horseless carriage was still a novelty, and a man and family simply could not travel far in comfortable fashion in a hack or surrey.

Mr. F. Kerble, lessee and manager of San Pedro Park, made a special effort to solicit the patronage of those in search of recreation of the better sort. A United States military band (Mr. Kerble advertised) would play at San Pedro every Sunday afternoon. There would also be choice music daily from 3:30 to 10:30 P. M., furnished very likely by musicians in the employ of the park manager. Mr. Kerble further declared that he could take care of parties, large or small, supplying them with refreshments, wines, music and "floor", "any time, on short notice". Nor was there

---

[30] *Evening Light* (April 29, 1884).

need to worry about the horses (the motive power of the vehicles), for patrons were "guaranteed" excellent stabling and good care of the same.[31]

Some pleasure-seekers, as did the Cumberland Presbyterian church members towards the latter part of April of 1884, spent the entire day on outings. The Presbyterians left town early and stayed long at the Second Mission (San José de Aguayo).[32] The season of picnics was indeed in full swing; the "Springs" (as San Pedro park was familiarly referred to) was "enlivened daily by the merry laugh and happy talk of the young people". On Friday the Public Schools would fill San Pedro to overflowing, a notice in the public press indicated.[33]

Such, we may presume, were the simple pleasures of young and old in the days before the automobile and movies. Railroads, in fact, were still a new-fangled means of travel and stage-coaches had not entirely passed from the scene. We can imagine that many readers of the *Evening Light* found great interest in an account of a trip which a reporter of that journal made over the "Sunset" from San Antonio to Brackett.[34]

The newsman took a ride on what was called the "Pacific extension" of the Sunset, leaving San Antonio at seven A. M. The train, pulling out from the railroad depot on Austin street, skirted the city at a snail's pace as it circled southward; then, after changing its direction of travel westward, it moved along at "three-cents-a-mile speed" for the whole day. Passengers had the pleasure of a view of the beautiful Medina Park before they were obliged to leave the cars for dinner at Sabinal. Twenty minutes were allowed for this function, the travellers having to stand in line on the platform in the hot sun while waiting for service.

At six P. M. the train reached Eagle Pass Junction. The Junction was made up of a collection of tents that housed a restaurant and drinking saloons. The *Light* representative joined other bold venturers on a further journey of eleven miles to Brackett. This

---

[31] *Ibid.* (April 22, 1884).
[32] *Ibid.* (April 28, 1884).
[33] *Ibid.*
[34] *Ibid.* (August 1, 1882).

distance he negotiated in a two-horse vehicle (which he failed to describe), under the direction of a Captain Bogle and a Mr. Newell. Brackett itself was nothing to speak of, but Fort Clark was so neat and attractive in appearance that the traveller felt amply rewarded for his trying 133-mile jaunt in the cars.[35]

One could still ride at that period on a four-horse Concord stage from San Antonio to Fredericksburg, by way of Leon Springs and Boerne. Coaches left from the Southwestern Stage Company agency at the Milburn Wagon Company building on Houston Street, "near the bridge", at 8 A. M. daily. W. F. Hansberger, superintendent, could assure patrons that there would always be responsible drivers to "hold the ribbons".[36]

It is not unlikely that among the travellers from San Antonio to Fredericksburg now and then there would be a salesman as "cheeky and fresh" as the character O. Henry tells us of whose business in life was the placing of Little Goliath windmills.[37] Sweet and Knox tell of a "soap drummer", a passenger on a coach travelling from Austin to San Antonio, who was prevented from committing the fatal error of wearing a plug hat into the Alamo City; but there is nothing in the behavior of this innocent to suggest the "aërial miller", Dunwoody of "The Sphinx Apple".

Whether there were any of the likes of Bildad Rose among the drivers of the Fredericksburg stage we can only surmise. The records of the transport phase of history of that period are scanty. One can reasonably suppose, however, that there were men of singular merit and distinction in control of the motive forces of those vehicles. Current in the "bullsessions" of the wagon-yards of South Flores in Santone, as late as the twenties of the present century, was a tale about a fabulous "holder of the ribbons" with the highly individualistic name of Bill. Bill, as the account has it, whipped his six-horse team down into Del Rio one day at dusk and brought the animals to his usual "classical" halt before the saloon doors of the stage station. Bill was down from the box and beside the bar with a big schooner of cool E. Anheuser beer

---

[35] *Ibid.*
[36] *Ibid.* (September 22, 1882).
[37] "The Sphinx Apple", *The Complete Works of O. Henry*, I, 211.

before a single passenger could emerge from the coach. But just as this jehu of the nopal and dust took his first sip of the brew, his off-wheeler, a flea-bitten sorrel of some years, dropped dead in the traces. Barflies, hangers-on, and patrons of repute gathered round Bill to taunt and "hurrah" him for letting a horse "fall in the traces", while he was controlling the ribbons. To allow a horse to commit such an indiscretion was considered a disgrace to the driver. But Bill was unperturbed by the words of his detractors. In a manner mindful somewhat of the deportment of Bret Harte's Yuba Bill, he calmly quaffed another modicum of his beer; then he mildly replied in his Southwestern drawl: "Hell, that hawse died ten miles back along the road, but I wouldn't let him fall till we reached this heah station."

It was a singular and distinctive age, that about which O. Henry wrote in his stories of the Southwest, but it was an age which the author knew as well, and interpreted as surely as Bret Harte did his times. It was an age that included what some have called the "mauve" decade, others the "yellow nineties", and still others the "gay nineties". Regardless of its colors and moods it certainly, like other eras, had its big moments and grand personages. And San Antonio was a "story city", in many ways just like any other city of comparable size in the land at that time, but in other respects as different as a city in a foreign land. Its picturesque little river, winding about its crooked streets and plazas and flat-roofed houses of stone and "dobe" gave this city of ozone and dust and sunshine a kind of Andalucian air that persists even to this day.

I

ALAMO PLAZA

Visitors to the Alamo in 1879 could well be both surprised and indignant at the condition in which they found the shrine of Texas liberty. This ancient church of the Mission of San Antonio de Valero at that time served as a warehouse to the adjoining general merchandise store of Honoré Grenet. The newspaper *The Surprise* (May, 1879) reported that a woman who entered the old chapel and stumbled over bags of salt and cans of kerosene was heard to remark that, "This takes all the romance out of the Alamo." And an old gentleman who, as a boy, had played on David Crockett's knee, was unable, because of great stacks of groceries, to find the spot where his hero had fallen.

Such a flagrant example of disrespect to the sacred shrine was made more noticeable by the wide variety of ways in which the name of the Alamo was kept green and fresh to the memory elsewhere in the city. San Antonio itself was commonly referred to as the "Alamo City"; a fashionable residence section at the headwaters of the San Antonio river was Alamo Heights; Alamo bottled beer was the "best beer brewed"; there was a barber shop called the Alamo Tonsorial Arena, as well as the Alamo Drug Store (a pharmaceutical shop which sold Alamo liniment and Alamo liver pills); the Alamo Flats were advertised as having forty "nicely furnished rooms, with electric bells, baths, etc., etc.,"; the Alamo Literary Society, mecca of culture and fashion, was housed in a two-story structure at the corner of Houston and Jefferson streets; and the Alamo Meat Market (a curious institution that aired its beef carcases from the eaves of a shop at the terminus of a street-car line at the south end of the Plaza) gave further prominence to the name of the noted chapel.[1]

Citizens with an orderly and mature conception of historical values, after years of agitation, prevailed upon the state legislature to buy the Alamo from its owners, the Roman Catholic Church authorities. A committee formed for the purpose negotiated the purchase of the building on May 26, 1883.[2] The price paid was $20,000.

At the time of Will Porter's arrival in Texas in 1882, a competent guide was on hand at the historic church to show visitors all the points of interest. With little trouble one could find the place where Bowie, ill of pneumonia, was murdered on his cot, the precise area where Travis drew his line, and the very spot where the intrepid Crockett satisfied the call of his destiny with the faithful Betsey in hand till the last.

The Plaza, itself, however, was still in a rough, unattended state. In dry seasons, it was an arid space with crater-like depressions half-filled with black gumbo dust or caliche powder; in the wet, the area became a loblolly of slush, abounding in chug-holes, or "abruptions", some of perilous depth. Sweet and Knox tell of how a wagon-load of U. S. Quartermaster depot employees suffered a bad spill when their vehicle struck one of the dust-filled "abruptions".[3] The span of Mexican mules pulling the wagon, animals skittish by nature anyhow, became excited at the confusion caused by the mishap and ran away, scattering passengers from one end of the plaza to the other. It was nothing unusual for a gang of rollicking cow-hands to have a frolic with an unwilling victim in the "arena" between the Alamo and Scholz's garden. One such band of fun-disposed "pokes", up from the brush country of the lower Nueces, playfully overtook and relieved a pair of fleeing Mexican fruit venders of their cart of apples right in the shadow of the Menger Hotel. Officers Brown, Chadwick and Mc Gorley, as representatives of law and order,

[1] "From where I stood I could see the Alamo livery-stable, the Alamo cigar-store, the Alamo tin-shop. I was told that around the corner I could find the Alamo bakery, the Alamo brewery, the engine-house of the Alamo Fire Company ...". (Sweet and Knox, *On a Mexican Mustang*, XXI, 187.)

[2] San Antonio *Express* (May 27, 1883).

[3] Sweet and Knox, *op. cit.*, XXXI, 401.

Alamo Plaza, showing Grenet's Castle, adjoining the Alamo.
Alamo Meat Market in Foreground.

pursued the cowmen and soon forced them to give up their ap-
propriation. The malefactors were arrested and placed under
bond. The next day, when it was revealed that the apple-peddlers
had stolen their wares, all parties involved were fined $25 and
released.[4] In much the same hilarious spirits as the "pokes" of this
incident, a band of O. Henry's cowboys rope and drag Curly the
tramp across the black soil of Military Plaza "until no respectable
rag-bag would have stood sponsor for his clothes".[5]

When Colonel Augustus Belknap and company (during the
winter of 1879) finished the street railway from San Pedro
Springs to the south corner of Alamo Plaza (the first carline in
the city, with mule-drawn vehicles), to keep the track out of the
mud it was found necessary to raise the rails two feet or more
along the entire course through the Plaza. This high ballast, however, while satisfying the designs of the railway, served both as a
barrier to cross traffic and as an impediment to the drainage of
the area it bisected. On September 7, 1882, six and a half inches
of rain, falling off and on all day long, put the entire region from
Grenet's Castle to the Alamo Market under water. A narrower
lake lay between the streetcar line and Scholz's Garden. While
perhaps the water was not over knee deep for the most part, in
the biggest chugholes a horse could sink to its belly. Once during
a heavy rain a beautiful bay animal was reported to have come
near drowning in a large slush-pit of stew-like density. And it is
likely that the creature would have drowned had not a buggy been
attached to it; the hole was simply too small to swallow up the
rig and its motive power together. The mules pulling the cars,
however, were able to trot merrily along on high ground, although
completely surrounded by the soupy inundation. Thus a provident
husband and father, buying two-bits worth of round steak at the
Alamo Market for supper, might, despite the flood, make his way
safely home to his wife and children with little or no delay –
unless perchance the carline crossed such a bridge as the new-
wrought iron structure on St. Mary's Street. It was at this point

---

4 San Antonio *Express* (August 31, 1883).
5 "The Higher Abdication", *Complete Works of O. Henry*, II, 995. Here-
after this full title will be abridged to the one word, *Works*.

that a large St. Bernard dog, attempting to cross the stream, was swept into the rampaging waters of the swollen San Antonio river.

The raising of the street-car line further emphasized the deplorable condition of the Plaza. The *Express* called the chugholes "abruptions", and surmised that citizens would have to endure these phenomena as permanent features of the landscape; *The Surprise* asked: "When will there ever be an end to the miserable, crude Indian village ideas that have obtained here ever since the intelligent, cultivated Spaniard disappeared?"

At the north end, the Plaza was dominated by the battlemented towers of the "inartistic erection" of Honoré Grenet; and at the south by a square brick and wood structure that housed the Alamo Meat Market.[6] The Menger Hotel overlooked the "dirty" expanse of the Plaza from the east side; across from the hostelry were several mercantile establishments, including G. B. Francis's clothing store. An advertisement in the *Light* of December, 1882, showed that this firm offered for sale a number of haberdashery items at attractive prices. Heavy winter suits were listed at $6.50; heavy ulster overcoats at $6.00; beaver overcoats at $4.50; shawls and skirts at 50 cents to $4.00; winter boots, $2.00; comforts, 75 cents.

Close by was Scholz's Palm Garden, a unique establishment that combined the essentials of both restaurant and recreation center. The place was advertised as a Paradise of Tropical plants, with three stories of airy galleries. At Scholz's, as the custom then was in the city, patrons rolled high dice to settle the score for drinks and rang for service a new-fangled contraption called an electric bell. There was an exquisite combination string and brass band to entertain guests while they sat at card tables in the semi-privacy of stalls or played at billiards in the large gameroom. In stall or in parlor, under brilliant incandescent lights, in this lovely center, with its setting of oleanders, palms, and cacti, the careworn visitor could recreate himself with the same degree of lavish elegance as that furnished in the patio of the Menger

---

[6]   William Corner, *San Antonio de Bexar, A Guide and History*, p. 144.

Hotel. Young Walter Goodall of Memphis, made beautiful by the god Phthisis, is drawn into one of these stalls by the smiles of a young woman, Miss Rosa. The two, one sick of body, the other, of mind, in these surroundings of happy promise, find solution to their worries.[7] Will Porter who tells of Goodall and Miss Rosa, would seem to have spent some time in Scholz's himself.

Dullnig's big grocery store at the corner of Alamo Plaza and Commerce street offered a wide selection of staple and fancy groceries to discriminating customers of the city. Every morning dapper salesmen in fashionable runabouts pulled by spirited ponies solicited orders among patrons on Laurel Heights, Tobin Hill, and Dignowity Hill. There were few articles in the grocery line that Dullnig could not supply to the meticulous patron.[8]

Up Commerce from Dullnig's, at 109 West, was the Harnish and Baer restaurant. It, too, like Scholz's, was decorated in the tropical manner. Banana trees grew in hot-house luxury down the center of the corridor of the ground floor. More restricted in its service to patrons than other eating-houses of the city, Harnish and Baer's offered the best Saint Louis and locally brewed beers, which its proprietor declared compared favorably with brews drunk in the rathskellers of München and Berlin.

A near neighbor to the Alamo chapel, the Menger Hotel, since its erection in 1859, had entertained a number of notable personages.[9] Among these were Sidney Lanier; Generals R. E. Lee, and U. S. Grant; Oscar Fingal O'Flahertie Wills Wilde, John McCullough, and other great actors; Thomas Wentworth Peirce, builder of the G. H. & S. A. railroad; as well as other railroad officials. Notable among the latter was Colonel P. B. Freer, a close associate of Colonel Peirce. Colonel Freer was the Sunset Route's city ticket agent. He made his home at the Menger.

[7] "A Fog in Santone", O. Henry, *Works*, II, 995.
[8] Material for Scholz's Garden and Dullnig's Grocery, as well as for Harnish and Baer, was furnished the writer by the late Julius Tengg. Mr. Tengg was for over seventy years a printer and stationer in San Antonio.
[9] This hotel was built by J. S. Kampmann for William A. Menger at an initial cost of $16,000.00. (William Corner, *op. cit.*, p. 147.) Frederick C. Chabot says that the "sum involved was $15,712.00, and that a later agreement increased the amount to $20,166.00". (Frederick C. Chabot, *With the Makers of San Antonio*, p. 406.)

Colonel Freer, on the eve of July 4, 1882, became the butt of a jest that would have been worthy of the fertile invention of Phonograph Davis, O. Henry's humorist of the Sut Lovingood stripe.[10] It had long been the custom of Colonel Freer to ride every day to the S. P. depot on Austin street in an old hack that was considerably the worse for age and wear. The two steeds that provided motive power for the old hack would have been fit teammates for Rocinante. The vehicle was driven by a "gemman of color", who appeared to be even more of an antique than the rig with whose custody he was entrusted. Business associates of Colonel Freer had dubbed the old Jehu General Brooks, and by this name he was known all over San Antonio. His features were more oriental than Congolese, although he was generally thought to be of the latter extraction. His eyes were small, dull, and lifeless; his ears were large – almost elephantine – and adorned with a pair of crude handmade earrings, objects of fairly large dimensions themselves.

Friends of Colonel Freer, thinking it beneath the dignity of the Southern Pacific ticket agent to ride to work in the dilapidated conveyance he made use of every day, found the old gentleman a respectable looking landau to replace his rickety carriage. Captains Thompson and Ned Howe made the presentation of the landau, captain Howe glorifying the occasion with befitting speech of somber tone and suitable length. Colonel Freer sat calmly with apparent unconcern through the whole ceremony, much to the chagrin of the perpetrators of the hoax; these gentlemen had expected an outburst of spleen from the curmudgeon. General Brooks, however, was experiencing noticeable agitation. His eyes, as small as they were, glowed like two little balls of fire; and a kind of smile, delicately etched, to be sure, but unmistakably real, stretched from earring to earring. He climbed down from his seat-box on the hack, unhitched his pair of rocinantes and in a short time had them coupled to the substitute vehicle. Colonel Freer, standing motionless all the while, appeared not the least bit moved by Ned Howe's eloquence. When Howe had concluded,

[10]   "The Marquis and Miss Sally", O. Henry, *Works*, II, 983.

the Colonel slowly climbed aboard the landau, and General Brooks ordered his charges to begin their daily trot to the Sunset Depot. Colonel Freer was as composed during the presentation rites as if the exchange of vehicles had been made on orders from his boss, Colonel Thomas Wentworth Peirce.[11]

T. W. Peirce, a frequent guest at the Menger, had won the esteem of San Antonians on the memorable fifteenth day of February, 1877. On that day his Galveston, Harrisburg & San Antonio railroad "really reached" San Antonio.[12] Three days before Christmas the *Express* had declared that track had been laid to Cibolo Creek, and was within twenty miles of the Alamo. The San Antonio construction company, a civic organization formed for the promotion of the railroad, at this time turned over to Colonel Peirce one-hundred thousand dollars in Bexar County bonds, as "per contract ratified by the citizens at an election some months ago". Several years were to elapse, however, before the Sunset was to join with the Southern Pacific to establish a through connection between New Orleans and San Francisco. This notable event occurred on January 13, 1883 (as is shown by the San Antonio *Express*, and Houston *Post* of date), at the Pecos River. Colonel Peirce and Major James Converse of the Sunset and Colonel Crocker and Mr. Spofford of the Southern Pacific took part in the ceremony of driving the silver spike. (On March 8, 1882, Colonel Peirce and Colonel Collis B. Huntington had met at the Menger Hotel to complete arrangements for the joining of the two segments of the transcontinental railway.)

Thomas W. Peirce's achievement in building the Galveston, Harrisburg & San Antonio railway was an act of greater im-

---

[11] Basic facts for this episode are taken from *The Surprise* newspaper of July 3, 1882. Supplementary material was furnished the writer by Julius Tengg and the late Wilmer Waldo of Houston. Mr. Waldo's father, J. Waldo, was vice-president of the Sunset at the time the incident referred to occurred. The San Antonio *Light* of January 17, 1885, reported Mr. Freer's death in the Lunatic Asylum at Austin. The gentleman was reported to have gone mad from drinking "loco weed tea."

[12] On February 5, 1877, a train had left San Antonio with U. S. Army officers as passengers for New York. (San Antonio *Express*, February 6, 1877.)

portance than he was ever given credit for. W. H. Osborne, president of the Illinois Central, congratulated Peirce at the time of the ceremony at the Pecos river, and declared that "he had overcome greater difficulties than the builders of the Union Pacific and other Pacific roads east of the Rockies. The money was out of Peirce's own pocket, and not from any delusive, ensnaring appeals to the public. The G. H. & S. A. has a safe, wide roadbed." [13]

Although, as the Galveston *News* said of Peirce at the time of his death (on October 2, 1885), "Every move he made was in his own interest", the man had a humanitarian side to his nature. His will shows that at his death he provided generously for hospitals and other buildings at the various towns along the route of the Sunset.[14] An interview which this very able rail developer granted a San Antonio *Light* reporter (December 13, 1882) was perhaps more revealing of his character than any of the numerous acts of the man's long business career. The interviewer of the journal comments that Peirce had the appearance of an "ideal hotel keeper". The Colonel he described as a tall, corpulent man, with a florid countenance and prominent veins which reminded the reporter of turtle soup and Piper Heidseick. The Colonel had a large head, with a shiny bald spot fringed with curling brown hair. He wore whiskers of a light color. A large double chin, with skin as soft as a child's, contrasted sharply with a myriad of little wrinkles that fanned out round his dull and steady blue eyes. He was dressed simply in a suit of "common" blue flannel. His watch was strung on a blue silk guard which lacked the usual gold clasp; his cuffs were fastened with cheap mother-of-pearl links, and even his black silk scarf had no ornament.

During the course of the interview he would now and then bridge his smallish nose with a pair of immense eye-glasses, an operation he performed with his excessively large and ink-stained hands.

The reporter asked Colonel Peirce if he had any idea of building a road to Fredericksburg. The Colonel thought that the con-

---

[13]   Galveston *News* (March 4, 1883).
[14]   See Appendix.

A Southern Pacific Ry. Train in the Eighties.

struction of such an extension would depend upon what inducements were offered. When asked his opinion about San Antonio's first class hotels, Peirce declared that he would "rather not answer that". He did add that "San Antonio is a very important sanitary point and should have good hotel accommodations."

Next there came a series of questions touching the Southern Pacific's relations with other railroads – the Texas Pacific and the Iron Mountain.

Reporter: "It is said that war has been declared against the Gould System and the Sunset by the Gulf, Colorado and Santa Fe. Is this true?"

Colonel Peirce: "It is not true. The relations are wholly amicable. There are a few differences regarding immaterial questions not affecting the general public."

When asked if there was a concert of action among railways in opposition to the three-cents-a-mile policy, Peirce was emphatic in stating that there was. He indicated that he and other officials would appear before the legislature to seek redress. And when asked if he considered the southwest a field for profitable investment, the Colonel declared that he definitely did. "But there will be no extension of railroads in Texas by me", he continued, "or by any one else connected with me, until the principle is asserted by the legislature that ownership of property – the ownership of railroads – gives control within the limits of the charter as in other property."

Peirce explained that his remarks were mainly in reference to the three-cents-a-mile policy, and the attempt to establish freight rates. He pointed out that no railroad in Texas paid dividends and that there was no likelihood that any one of them would ever do so. Since there are no navigable rivers in Texas, and no other way than with railroads to make the state a commercial and agricultural center, "If you stop railroads the population of the state will in a year recede to 200,000."

Colonel Peirce then left the Menger Hotel lobby, pulled himself up into a hack and was driven to the Sunset depot on Austin street. Here he boarded his $25,000 private car – the same car in which he had travelled with General Sherman and Collis P.

Huntington less than a year before – and soon was on his way to the west coast.[15]

Another Menger Hotel guest at this period, and one who certainly must have made an impression on the populace of the city, was Oscar Wilde. Wilde gave a lecture entitled "Decorative Art" (so the *Evening Light* reported) at the Turner Hall, on June 22, 1882. The newspaper said of Wilde that he had a face "distinguished in feature, exhibiting decided force of character, combined with considerable indication of nervous temperament, which is toned and *effemitised* by his long, rough hair, which falls upon his shoulders".

The lecturer wore a black velvet suit, of perhaps an eighteenth-century design, with breeches gartered at the knees, silk stockings and low shoes with buckles. Nothing was said of the yellow sunflower that usually adorned the great Irishman's coat lapel; perhaps the floral addition had become such an indispensable item of his dress that it was not thought worthy of comment.

Wilde began his lecture by saying that he was going to speak on the positive beauties of art and to tell what use his countrymen were making of art in the improvement of handicraft in England. He defined decorative art as "joy all round, in which the worker shares and produces better art". A well-done piece of work, he declared, shows that the workman who made it used his head and heart as well as his hands.

The lecturer was frank and even venturesome in his criticism of San Antonians, Texans, and, by extension, of all Americans. "You do not honor art sufficiently", he told his audience: "nor will you do so until you can see that there is no nobler profession for your son to learn than the creation of the beautiful." He told his listeners that, although they considered themselves a great

---

[15] Thomas Wentworth Peirce came to Texas in 1842. He was among the first Northern business men to see the possibilities for the development of the Lone Star State. From 1847 till the beginning of the Civil War, he maintained a fleet of twelve to fourteen ships plying between Boston, Galveston, and Liverpool. After the War he became interested in railroads, an interest that resulted in the building of the Galveston, Harrisburg and San Antonio. Colonel Peirce (the name was sometimes spelled Pierce) was sixty-eight years old when he died. (Galveston *News*, October 4, 1885).

nation, he could not think them really so. It is a common experience in America, he declared, to see "ill-proportioned houses, wretched wall papers, and badly worn carpets". He singled out for attack "that monstrosity, the cast iron stove". He said he could perhaps tolerate the stove, "if you would not decorate it". The festooned base and the "funeral urn" surmountings he found particularly objectionable.

Americans, he said he had observed, put undue emphasis on the term "second-hand"; it had become the most "uneuphonious" of all words in use. Simply because a thing is second-hand should not mean that it is of less value than when new. For instance, a piece of furniture well designed and well made should gain rather than lose value with age. Wilde advised San Antonio listeners to encourage their young people to learn and practice art. They must not, he said, send to New York and pay heavily for goods which do not suit them and which do not satisfy their tastes. They should instead learn to weave their own carpets, design their own furniture and make their own pottery.

The essence of the lecturer's concluding remarks was that art is based on sincerity and truth. If a child learns nature he will want to make better use of it than "throwing a stone at it". "You of the South", he declared, "with your wonderful surroundings of nature should have perfect art." The development of railways and steamship lines should bring material wealth, but Wilde counselled that the "independence of art is the perfect expression of freedom".

Alamo Plaza was still in the mud when the new Grand Opera house first opened its doors on December 20, 1886.[16] The sumptuous playhouse was to take the place of Turner Opera Hall (on Houston street, at the intersection of St. Mary's) as San Antonio's leading theatre.

The Grand of San Antonio had a fairly commodious stage. The width of the proscenium opening was thirty-two feet; the height was thirty feet; the distance from footlights to the back wall was forty feet. These dimensions compared favorably with those of

[16]   Mesquite block pavement was first laid in the Plaza in 1889.

the Hollis theatre of Boston. In the Boston playhouse the width of the proscenium opening was thirty-eight feet; the height, forty feet; and the distance from the footlights to the back wall was fifty-five feet.[17] The drop curtain had been painted by Nixon, Toomey and Albert, noted scene designers of Chicago. The architect was M. McElfatrick of Saint Louis.

Thomas W. Mullally was lessee of the building; Colonel H. P. Andrews, "capitalist and large property owner", was president; William Aubrey was vice president; and Colonel John Withers, cashier of the San Antonio National Bank, was treasurer. Ernest Riche, well known in theatre circles of the city by reason of his long connection with Turner Hall, was engaged as manager. The directors (the *Express* said) were Judge T. J. Devine, Colonel Augustus Belknap, Colonel Uriah Lott, W. H. Maverick, Colonel J. B. Lacoste, and C. K. Brenerman.

Emma Abbott, America's popular native born prima donna, hurried to the city by special train from Taylor to christen the Grand with a performance of the opera *Lucretia Borgia*. Miss Abbott had had to put up with the inconvenience of three train wrecks after leaving Omaha on her way to Taylor; and her late arrival at San Antonio delayed the start of the performance until three minutes to nine.[18] During this initial presentation, three hundred of the "gallery gods" indulged in their usual whistling and stamping of feet, thereby (as the newspaper the *Express* observed) putting the new opera house to a severe test. The audience generally was stiff and cold (a *Light* reporter declared), perhaps because of the strangeness of the new surroundings. But Miss Abbott herself gave one of the fine performances that had endeared her to opera-lovers in the "provinces". An unusually eager *Express* representative talked to Miss Abbott between acts.

"What do I think of the house?" she said, in response to his question. "Only one thing to think. It's a beauty. I am tired of chocolate colored opera houses. Five out of six I've opened are

---

[17] Julius Cahn, *Theatrical Guide*, Vol. III.
[18] Emma Abbott had christened more opera houses in the U. S. than any other star. (Sadie E. Martin, *Life and Professional Career of Emma Abbott*, XIII, 98.)

done in what are known as aesthetic tints. That is, they are neutral and dull. There's a brightness about this that's inspiring and charming."

And then Miss Abbott, who was noted among the divas of that era for the care she exercised in her dress, said to the *Express* reporter, "Do you like my crown? It was made for my Washington debut as Semiramide. It's not really a stage jewel, you know. These large stones pendant are diamonds." (She must have indicated the objects she referred to by touching them.) "This one weighs eight carats. The filigree is of gold."

Miss Abbott was exuberant. Perhaps the capacity crowd lifted up her spirits – although as America's favorite prima donna she was accustomed to "standing room only" situations.

"I was so afraid that we wouldn't be here on time", she hastily added. She looked at a clock in her dressing room as she spoke. Time was passing. The curtain for the second act would soon go up. "I was anxious to do my best for them and so I told my company. There is not one who is not doing all he or she knows how. I take great pride in my people. Just wait till you hear Lizzie's solo in the next act."

That was Emma Abbott. She was referring to an associate in her company, Lizzie Annandale. And Lizzie did give an impressive exhibition of her voice; and so did Montegriffo, leading tenor of the troupe. Montegriffo who "gets the high *C* all the way through – not *B* flat – the high *C*". But Emma shone brilliantly; she surpassed them all.

O. Henry was to write of Miss Abbott in a letter from Austin, December 22, 1885.

Emma sang finely. I applauded at the wrong times, and praised her rendering of the chromatic scale when she was performing on "c" flat andante pianissimo, but otherwise the occasion passed without anything to mar the joyousness of the hour.[19]

Miss Abbott felt that she "owed it" to her audiences to present herself in as grand a manner as possible. The crown with the eight carat diamond is a case in proof of this. She was reputed to have

[19]   O. Henry, *Works*, II, 1079.

spent $200,000 for a season's wardrobe; the noted designers, Felix and Worth of Paris, regularly made her dresses. She wore gorgeous costumes, all Worth creations, as Marie Theresa, Queen of Spain, in *Ruy Blas*, her second night's offering. Her first dress, (as an Express account informs us), had a groundwork of silvery white moire antique; and in the second act, she wore a gown with a front of amber velvet, the sides of ruby, and the train a combination of the two colors. Over all was a network of silver pearls, which greatly enhanced the brilliancy of the ensemble. With this dress she wore the royal mantle, bordered with a deep band of ermine, and extending for yards over the gown's massive train. With both dresses, Miss Abbott wore a charming tiara, studded with rubies, opals, sapphires, and diamonds.[20]

Prices of seats for the Abbott engagement ranged from $2 for the parquette and parquette circle to fifty cents for the gallery.[21]

Another notable to visit the New (later the Grand) Opera House that season was the tragedian Edwin Booth. The name of this great actor was familiar in every household at the time; O. Henry, in a letter to Dr. W. P. Beall, jokingly refers to Booth as a probable portrayer of a rôle in a play he had written.[22] Booth was to tell his friend Horace Howard Furness that he had found the hotels and theatres in Texas excellent and the "audiences very cultured and in full dress".[23] At San Antonio Booth gave up a planned afternoon drive in the parks to play at a matinée for a guarantee of $3000, a sum that would pay for the hire of his private railroad car, *The David Garrick,* from that city to San Francisco.[24] The great player, however, did take time out to visit the Alamo. The *Light* reported that Booth visited the shrine shortly after his arrival and was conducted through the building and premises by custodian Tom Rife. The actor seemed quite an absorbed and interested observer and asked many questions.

[20] Sadie E. Martin, *op. cit.,* V, 46.
[21] On Christmas day of this year (1886), Adelina Patti stopped over in San Antonio for twenty minutes. The diva was on her way to Mexico City after an engagement at Galveston. (San Antonio *Express,* December 26, 1886.)
[22] O. Henry, *Works,* II, 1072.
[23] Edwina Booth Grossman, *Recollections of Edwin Booth,* page 271.
[24] Katherine Goodale, *Behind the Scenes with Edwin Booth,* XVII, 132.

Grand Opera House. San Antonio, 1895.

A *Light* dramatic critic, after witnessing Booth's presentation of *Richelieu*, wrote that he had seen Macready, Sam Phelps, Charles Kean, Tommaso Salvini, Lawrence Barrett, Henry Irving, W. Creswick, John McCullough, Frederick Warde, and Tom Keene – "and with all these, Booth makes a fair comparison". Booth has defects, he admitted, but his defects are overshadowed by the "general brilliance of his impersonation". An orchestra from the Eighth Cavalry band, increased to thirteen pieces for the occasion, played some remarkably fine music during the afternoon performance of *Richelieu*.

The proceeds of the two performances (Saturday, February 26, 1887: *Richelieu*, matinée; *Hamlet*, evening) were in excess of $6000, a "take" that we may suppose had something to do with making the player conscious of culture in Texas.

The tragedian was to return to the Grand the next season (February, Wednesday and Thursday, the 22nd and 23rd, 1888) in company with Lawrence Barrett. The famous player-partners appeared on successive evenings in *Othello* and *Julius Caesar*. Tickets for the two performances went on sale at the Grand box-office on the seventeenth. The *Express* reported that the sidewalk in front of the Opera House was overflowing with eager ticket-buyers from early morning till night. "On all sides could be heard the rustle of currency and jingle of silver and gold." When the box-office closed, Dr. Teele (theatre-manager Rische's assistant) had taken in $4,700. The *Express* was proud of this figure. "The $5,500 taken in Dallas", the journal declared, "was for three performances – as also was the $4,400 taken in Galveston."

The great enthusiasm of the playgoers of San Antonio and elsewhere in the Southwest at that time speaks well for the refined tastes of the people of that region. A reader of the present time can understand the ardent interest of those Texans of an earlier day if he bears in mind the bubbling zeal of the crowds who gather nowadays to hear and see the Beatles perform.

The *Express* headlined its account of the Booth and Barrett *Othello* with these words: Two Giant Representatives of American Art in the Event of the Season. And of Booth's Iago, it said: "What is there to be said about it? Bristling with that subtlety of conception which genius alone can give. It is needless to dwell upon it." Nor was Barrett slighted in deference to his renowned rival. His Othello was called a "gem in declamatory talent". One might deduce from this that Barrett's Moor was on the John Phillip Kemble order. The appraiser declared further that the conception was lacking in the easy grace "which marks the every motion and voice infection of Edwin Booth".

Of the performance of *Julius Caesar* the following night the reviewer admitted his inability to write with the proper critical acumen. He did imply that he considered the tragedy "cut up". He thought Barrett tried to give the audience his very best interpretation of Cassius, but Booth was thought to be careless, although "apparently content to speak his lines as only Booth can". *Othello* and *Julius Caesar* both were standing-room-only performances.

An actress of the grand manner, whose favorite rôle was Schiller's Marie Stuart in a play by that name, was Mrs. D. P. Bowers. Mrs. Bowers visited San Antonio early in January of 1887. The actress declared in an interview at the outset of her stay that she was an American and that all her dresses were American made. "No Worth creations for me." Her company, too, she declared, were American. "I love them and they love me." Mrs. Bowers could have been making a few thrusts at Emma Abbott. In response to the *Light* reporter's asking her how she liked the state, she replied that the cordiality of the people endeared Texas to her. She was on her first visit, but the visit would certainly not be her last. Said Mrs. Bowers:

The high state of musical and dramatic culture that I find here surprises me much, and proves how much Texas is misrepresented and misunderstood in the northern and eastern cities. The usual idea there is that a Texan is a savage and a desperado armed with a revolver and a bowie knife.

She concluded her remarks by saying that she had met no savages yet, but had seen "as fine and as cultured gentlemen as ever graced a New York or Boston house".

Edwin Booth, when writing of his tour through Texas sometime prior to Mrs. Bower's visit, had said: "Cow-boys, cactus and greasers are plentiful thereabouts; but from what I saw of them, I should say the cactus is the most dangerous of the three nuisances." [25] That such a notion of the wild nature of Texas was current in the North and East was indicated by other players who visited the state during that era. Fanny Davenport, who had been a frequent visitor at Turner Opera House, had told a Galveston interviewer how she had been wholesomely disillusioned on her tour of the state. "Divine" Fanny said that she was disappointed in not seeing "a terrible slaughter of people, drawn knives, and huge Colt revolvers and long hair and green-eyed monsters".[26] Mrs. Langtry had left her jewels in New Orleans for fear of being robbed. When her private car, the "Lalee", was jolted off the rails at a small town west of San Antonio, the "dreadful cowboys" whom she had professed such a great fear of entertained her with an improvised tournament, nowadays called a rodeo.[27] O. Henry makes Octavia Beaupree's Aunt Ellen refer to a Texas ranch as a place occupied by centipedes, fandangos, and cowboys. The last, she had heard, were devils incarnate. How much more to be dreaded a fandango or a centipede must be! The ranch which her niece's husband has left her she declares is more of a liability than an asset.[28] It is not without cause that Chicken Ruggles steps cautiously through the pasture of curly mesquite grass, afraid of all that he might meet in the wilderness — snakes, brigands, centipedes, mirages and cowboys.[29] Chicken had read his paper on the park bench and knew that a man afoot was more liable to an attack from the varmints of the desert than an actress riding through in the luxury of a private car.

By the end of the century, Alamo Plaza had undergone a change that was little short of miraculous. The metamorphosis of this public square could be likened fittingly to a stage-setting of a luxurious palace garden that had taken the place of the squalid slums of a great city in a "transformation" act in the most lurid

25 Edwina Booth Grossman, *op. cit.*, p. 270.
26 Joseph S. Gallegly, *Footlights on the Border*, VIII, 112.
27 Lillie Langtry, *The Days I Knew*, XI, 189.
28 "Madame Bo Peep of the Ranches", *Works*, II, 1240.
29 "The Passing of Black Eagle", *Works*, I, 432.

of the "sensation" melodramas of that period. In the first place, the Plaza had been lifted out of the mud – which is to say, it had also been taken out of the dust. A beautiful garden of native flowers, an ellipse in shape, with a protecting curb, occupied a great part of the space between the Menger Hotel and the Grand Opera House. A smaller garden, in the form of a circle and tastefully planted, was at the north end of the area near the new post office and federal building. In the midst of this smaller setting stood a bandstand, with a canopy not unlike the tower of a Turkish mosque. Here on selected evenings interested listeners found relaxation in the music of a brass band that played Strauss waltzes and Mexican *canciones de amor*.

The imposing façade of the Grand Opera House building dominated the side of the Plaza opposite the Menger Hotel. In this structure, besides the theatre, were the rooms of the San Antonio Club, an institution which was founded for "literary purposes, to promote social intercourse among its members and to provide them the convenience of a club house". It was said of this fraternal association that "its receptions were among the great social functions of the city".[30] While this remark is very likely true, it is doubtful if any of these entertainments were more literary in character than social. Since many of the directors of the Club were also members of the Opera House board it may be presumed that the playhouse satisfied the cultural demands of the Club members.

Harnish and Baer's restaurant, its splendor perhaps a bit tarnished since earlier days, still had about it a dignity and old-world atmosphere that seemed to grow more wholesome with the passage of years. On March 5, 1888, the San Antonio Division Uniform Rank of the Knights of Pythias honored at this popular eating house a distinguished fellow-Pythian, the tragedian Frederick Warde. The dinner took place at half past eleven at night; it was scheduled at that time because the honoree's notable presentation of *Galba, the Gladiator* had occupied the earlier part of the evening. It was Warde's robustness and vigor of style, which he

---

[30]   William Corner, *op. cit.*, page 41.

displayed to great advantage as Galba, that had endeared him to San Antonio audiences. Warde was more popular in the city than was Tom Keene, the provincial exponent of Shakespeare, whose musical voice and facial contortions had made him a great rival of the Englishman. It is not amiss to note, however, that Warde's assumption (in the evening following his *Galba*) of Celia Logan's adaptation of *Gaston Cadol* (if we are to believe the *Express*) many playgoers simply could not abide. Declared the journal:

The idea of a man, and he a warrior, loving to distraction a woman who hates him, and persists in and insists on hating him, is preposterous. In the brain of no man could be born such a simpering idiot and egregious ass as Celia Logan and Frederick Warde, either jointly or separately, make of Gaston.

According to reports in both the *Light* and the *Express*, the dinner tendered Warde must have gone off smoothly. The player was eulogized by past chancellor Ramsay, Captain George R. Dashiell, and F. H. Bushick. The honoree himself told of the changes that had taken place in the city since his first appearance at the Casino Hall ten years before. At that time he came into the city on the Austin-San Antonio stage. He implied likewise that acting was somewhat of a hazardous business in Austin in those days. At the Capital City he had had a frightening experience. It happened in this wise. He was playing Iago to the Othello of the late tragedian John McCullough at the Millet opera house. In the morning after the performance a newspaper editor called on Warde to tell him how he had saved his life the night before. The editor told the story of a man from the country who was unfamiliar with the art of make-believe, and had never seen *Othello* presented on the mimic stage before. This gentleman had mistaken the play-acting villainy of Warde's Iago as the behavior of a real scoundrel deadbent on putting the horns on an innocent husband. As Iago continued to enmesh the general in his fabric of lies about the chastity of Desdemona, the country playgoer began to rise in his seat, declaring that if that son of a bitch did not leave the poor husband alone he would let him have a couple of slugs from his forty-five. He was unlimbering his artillery to put his threat into effect when the editor (who sat behind the badly deceived gentleman) with a timely restraining gesture probably saved the actor's life. Warde said that while of course he appreciated the would-be avenger's compliment to the realism of his portrayal of the ancient, he could not help feeling more grateful to the editor for saving him from an awkward and embarrassing position.[31]

[31] Frederick Warde, *Fifty Years of Make Believe*, XV, 192.

II

HOUSTON STREET AND BEYOND

At the turn of the century – and even until 1910 – Grenet's wooden monstrosity, the castle-like travesty, still sullied the dignity of the Plaza with its obtrusiveness, unwelcomed and condemned, a monument to the pertinacity of the "mossbacks". By 1889, the new federal building, which housed the federal courts and post office, an imposing mass of hewn limestone, had taken its place at the north end of the Plaza.[1] The structure was called by some a "medieval dream", and did embody in its composition many of the elements of a Rhine castle. It had a tower, and a turret, and an arcade along its façade. Originally projected by architect M. E. Bell of Chicago, the building was modified in design and finished by W. A. Freret of New Orleans during Cleveland's first term of office. The structure was perhaps more fittingly characterized as being of the Richardson Romanesque style of architecture.[2]

Before Cleveland's elevation to the Presidency, the position of postmaster of the San Antonio district had been a matter of bitter dispute among aspirants for the office. In July of 1882 James P. Newcomb, editor of the *Evening Light* newspaper, was appointed to the position. The *Express*, a Democrat paper, called the elevation of Newcomb "a mild outrage against the people of San Antonio", but Republicans of the city regarded the appointment as a victory for them, for no local man since the termination of the "late unpleasantness" had been given consideration for the

---

[1] *San Antonio Express* (May 6, 1889).
[2] William Corner, *San Antonio de Bexar*, p. 39.

lucrative post.[3] It developed, however, that the local powers were "too soon elate"; before Newcomb could take office, P. M. Manning, who had long held the position as deputy for a Mrs. Norris of St. Louis, went to Washington and succeeded in nullifying Newcomb's claim.[4] With Grover Cleveland as chief executive (in 1885) a Democrat gained the coveted post, thereby establishing a short era of home rule in the handling of the mail.

The street railway companies during the period had modernized and expanded their services. The Belknap line, now electrified, ran out to the three railroad depots: out Avenue C to the Southern Pacific on Austin street; along Dolorosa street to the International and Great Northern; and to the San Antonio and Aransas Pass out South Flores street. The Army Post on Government Hill, and Muth's beer garden, a favorite spot in that locality, were also served by the Avenue C line. A line also headed out Soledad street to Laurel Heights and San Pedro Park, a fashionable residence section and the most popular recreation area in the city. In 1880, Brackenridge Park, a gift to the city from Colonel George W. Brackenridge, was opened to the public. Because of its large size and scenic beauty, this handsome wooded area soon took the place of San Pedro as the most popular resort for pleasureseekers. Steam cars from Milam Square could reach Brackenridge in ten minutes.

Just prior to the opening of Brackenridge (in May of 1879), the newspaper *Surprise*, in speaking of the San Antonio river, complained that "our beautiful little river is gradually becoming the sewer of the city". Dams along its course, the journal said, had resulted in big accumulations of filth. A few lazy prisoners pulled grass out of the water once in a while, but it would take a scow and two huskies with rakes really to clean out the stream. It was said that a gentleman reported finding in the river, in one week's time, between the Lewis mill on Garden street and the Houston street bridge, "one dead horse, one dead two-year-old cow, five dogs, nine cats, and chickens and cats without number, and by stirring up the sediment a most odious stench is turned

[3]   *San Antonio Express* (July 1, 1882).
[4]   *San Antonio Light* (July 5, 1882).

loose". All these details of the pollution of the pretty little meandering stream were faithfully recorded as a public service by the *Surprise*.

By the middle nineties Alamo Plaza, as well as parts of Houston and Commerce Streets, had been paved with octagon-shaped blocks of mesquite wood.[5] This material seemed durable enough and was soft and easy on horses' hooves in the temperate seasons, but in hot weather the blocks showed a tendency to swell and buckle. The caliche surface forming a base for the pavement became at this time powdery and cancerous with spongy depressions. In very cold weather, too, Mexican urchins would come out of their jacals in the west end of town and carry blocks back into their homes for firewood. This practice of the little Latin boys in rustling stove-wood often resulted in the making of chug-holes or "abruptions" not unlike those which in former days had been such a source of annoyance to unwary horses and foot-passengers who travelled about on the dirt surfaces of the unpaved thoroughfares.[6]

In September, when the rains came (the Alamo City was subject to autumnal deluges), the mesquite chunks swelled and formed undulations that were hazards to both man and beast. A person of historical bent might like to speculate on how well the eight-sided mesquite blocks would have withstood such a flood as that which inundated downtown San Antonio on September 7, 1882. On that date six and a half inches of rain fell within a span of ten hours. A muddy lake, not so deep as a well but fully as wide as a church door, formed on Alamo Plaza, making that region look pretty much as it had in the days of the Old Regime and fully as hazardous as it anciently had been to all but the most nimble and wary wanderers. Main and Military plazas at the time were knee-deep in murky pools of litter and debris. In Navarro and St. Mary's streets, where those travel-ways crossed the river, water was several inches deep and the mud inches deeper. A large collie dog was swept away as it attempted to cross St. Mary's bridge,

[5] Wooden block pavement was first laid at 828 Avenue D by Walter Scott, May 17, 1882.
[6] From the recollections of the writer's aunt, Mrs. E. W. Pells.

the *Light* reported. The Vance hotel, on the site of the present Gunter, had a foot of water covering its ground floor; and two blocks further north on this same St. Mary's, at the residence of Dr. E. B. Rankin, two horses were found swimming in the back yard; the doctor was able to save one, but the other drowned. When the flood had subsided, in San Pedro creek bodies of cows, horses and burros were found in numbers along its banks.

Although most of the principal downtown streets of the city had been paved by the late nineties, sidewalks as a rule were left pretty much as the Canary Island founders had made them, and this despite a city ordinance enacted to enforce improvement in these pavements. The *Surprise*, (a journal which seemed never to tire of suggesting reforms) spoke of the "old style Mexican sandstone mosaic walks that never wear out, but wear out plenty of shoe-leather every year". These walks, the newspaper observed, are a disgrace to a civilized community. "It makes little difference to the already grown San Antonians, who go shuffling along in the most ungraceful style; but it is a downright shame to tolerate a condition that will ruin the style and gait of the children." [7]

The Maverick Bank, with Samuel A. Maverick as proprietor and L. W. Menger as cashier, occupied a handsome building of five stories catercornered from the Post Office. It was a red brick structure of unusual design, with a mansard roof and balconies on the Houston street and Alamo Plaza sides of each story.[8] Mr. Maverick had given land to the Government for the Post Office and it would appear that with his new building he was acting to keep abreast of the trend to improve the appearance of his part of the city. As a further sign of his wish to enhance the looks of the region he had added to and done over his building at the intersection of Jefferson and Houston streets and reopened the place as a hotel.[9] This alteration he completed on April 29, 1882, and by 1890 the hostelry was next in importance to the Menger itself.

The Alamo Literary Society, as early as 1872, had erected a spacious hall of two stories on a large lot given the organization

---

[7] *The Surprise*, Vol. 1, No. 2 (July, 1879).
[8] Corner, p. 142.
[9] *Ibid.*

Houston Street, looking west, *circa* 1882. Alamo Society Literary Hall on Right.

by Mr. Maverick.[10] This land is at the north corner of Jefferson and Houston streets, directly across from the Maverick hotel.[11] The building put up at that time was of limestone and brick, with a roof of cedar shingles. The upstairs section contained an auditorium and stage; neither was especially large, although adequate for most of the organization's demands. Members of the Society were drawn from the most respectable people of the city, chiefly from the German and Anglo-American, which, in the eighties, were the two main elements of the population. For a pastime in a cultural way, the gentleman members of this club would indulge in debate, quite often on questions pertaining to the use of liquor and tobacco; and their wives, auxilliary members, read poetry and reviewed novels, and played euchre. Owen Meredith's *Lucile* is a longer poetical effusion that engaged the attention of the women.[12] In the matter of added amusement neither sex, it would appear, was opposed to the idea of witnessing a vaudeville act or so now and then, on their own stage, provided the players conducted themselves with the proper restraint offstage, and Mr. Jack Harris of the Vaudeville Theatre was in a mood to allow his practitioners of song and dance to exhibit their wizardry at the more genteel establishment on Houston street. Women of the top circles simply would not enter the portals of the "Vaudeville" itself, although their husbands, impelled by an exploratory urge, might once in a while hazard a venture into the customary haunts of the frolicsome "ponies". When the box-office till of the Vaudeville began to reflect a decline in patronage, Mr. Harris quite often felt disposed to make a concession to the wishes of the more refined element of the merriment-seekers of the city.

On an occasion early in the history of the Hall, when Miss Mollie Sommers was the toast of Main Plaza (which is to say, of the White Elephant Saloon), the whole strength of the Vaudeville

[10] *Ibid.*, p. 131.
[11] The San Antonio City Directory of 1879-80 lists the Alamo Literary Hall at the corner of Houston and Jefferson streets as one of the amusement halls of the city.
[12] Partly from the reminiscences of Julius Tenngg.

Theatre company was carried over to the Alamo Hall – the entire coterie of players together with Professor Ohse and his brass band of ten pieces. (The playhouse was then under the management of D. G. Bronson.) Long before curtain time all the seats at the Alamo auditorium were filled. One might say that the whole strength of the Society had gathered in the hopes of gaining glimpses into the far reaches of the nether world. Some, we fancy, indulged in idle chat, but many must have sat nervously and fearful as they waited for the curtain to rise; after so long a time it did rise; and presently there appeared Miss Mollie Sommers, the particular star of the Carlotta Comedy Troupe, as lustrous and appealing as Lydia Thompson or Anna Held.[13] It was soon clear that the amiable artiste was delighting rather than shocking the sensibilities of the most fastidious of the auditory; it would not be an untruth to state that Miss Sommers had extended her circle of admirers of the music-loving public with pleasing renditions of the lady's two great hit numbers, the songs, "Not If the Court Knows Itself", and "Shaking Dices". Both pieces were of Professor Ohse's own composition. (O. Henry's Cisco Kid is familiar with the first song of the Professor; he tells Tonia, "Not if the court knows itself do I let a lady stake my horse for me.")[14]

The main attraction for the occasion of which we now speak was the comedy drama, *Naval Engagements*, a piece written by the popular English playwright, Charles Dance. Miss Carlotta was starred in this play as Mary Mortimer, the young girl to whom the much older Admiral Kingston is betrothed. John A. Stevens assumed the part of Admiral Kingston, and Viola May that of

[13] Lydia Thompson, a popular English burlesque performer, made her debut in New York in 1868, in *Ixion*. She introduced burlesque to the United States, "with all its allurements of shapely forms, blonde wigs, 'wocal welvet'". *Lurline*, or *The Knights of the Naiads*, and *Sinbad, the Sailor*, were two of her best known numbers. H. P. Phelps, *Players of a Century* (2nd ed.), XXVII, 381.

Anna Held, French musical comedy star of "wicked, self-conscious, sensuous beauty", was to make a hit in San Antonio in 1890 with her "coon" song, "I Want Them Presents Back". J. S. Gallegly, *Footlights on the Border*, XII, 166.

[14] O. Henry, "The Caballero's Way", *Works*, I, 207.

Mrs. Pontifex. J. G. Steele played the role of Lieutenant Kingston. The olio that followed the comedy was "select and unequalled", as the bills of the day had it. Mr. Stevens gave a recitation, "Thomas O'Brien"; Miss Viola May recited, "You and I"; and Miss Carlotta herself rendered, "When Charlie Plays the Drum".[15] The whole concluded with a "Ne plus ultra clock-work double jig" by Miss May Olive and Johnny Pierce.

The Vaudeville company in its own playhouse had been advertised shortly before as having the best Dutch comedians, the best clog and jig dancers, the best banjoist, the best Ethiopian comedian, a ventriloquist (not denominated as the best), and Mr. Johnnie C. Smith, a singer and dancer, who could "elicit more applause than he could stand".[16] However, besides their excellence in the qualities they professed, many of these performers could do very well in interpreting roles in drama of a finished kind. Charles Dance's *Naval Engagements* is a case illustrative of this exercise of talent. The two-act comedy was at the time meeting with wide acceptance both in the United States and Britain. Horace and Alice Dunning Lingard, English players of note, had toured Texas a few years before with *Naval Engagements* and another Dance comedy, *Delicate Ground*, in their repertory; their success with the plays in Texas had done much to popularize the two dramas. Of course one can hardly say that Miss Carlotta was an Alice Dunning Lingard, certainly not in talent, even if in looks; but there is no reason to suppose that the variety performer was not capable of a "sound" performance. Certainly she had a creditable vehicle and she is to be commended for making a fine selection. Dance's *comedietta*, *Delicate Ground*, prompted the following remark from Allardyce Nicoll: "... it is not too much to say that in Dance we have the far-off ancestor of Bernard Shaw".[17]

A sketch of the plot of *Naval Engagements* will be of value in

[15] *Olio*, derived from the Spanish *olla* (an earthenware pot of meat and vegetables), was commonly employed in 19th-century variety show circles as a synonym for programme or bill. For a detailed account of the origin and history of this word, see the *Oxford Shorter Dictionary*.

[16] *Express* (January 19, 1875).

[17] Allardyce Nicoll, *A History of English Drama*, IV, 126.

helping the reader understand the comedy San Antonians witnessed on the occasion in question.

At the beginning of the piece (I, i) we find Lieutenant Kingston, Royal Navy, in a predicament. He is a guest at the Fountain Inn at Portsmouth, whence he has just arrived from duty in Gibraltar. With him is the pretty widow, Mrs. "Colonel" Pontifex, to whom he is engaged to marry. The lady is fifteen years older than he. The two are unquestionably in love, as their actions and words show. But Kingston, as he explains to Mrs. Pontifex, finds himself in a grave difficulty. He tells her that two years ago, shortly before he left England for Gibraltar, he had discussed the subject of marriage with his widower father, Admiral Kingston:

We entered into an engagement that neither of us was to marry a woman of an age unsuitable to his own; this, little thinking into whose delightful society I was going to be thrown, I, in a moment of indiscretion, agreed to.

To render the situation more confusing, his father in the meantime has become engaged to the son's childhood playmate, Mary Mortimer. The girl is thirty years the Admiral's junior. By a rare coincidence, both couples are lodging at the Fountain, their presence at first unknown to one another. By the end of the first act, the audience perceives that there is but one way to resolve the complications: the father and son must exchange fiancées; and this of course is precisely what does occur.

The awkwardness that arises from the wide difference in age between Lieutenant Kingston and his older fiancée furnishes the occasion for some amusing dialogue. Here is a sample:

Mrs. Pontifex. A penny for your thoughts, Kingston dear.
Lieut. Kingston. They're not worth it.
Mrs. P. Then you ought to be ashamed of yourself, for you can't have been thinking of me.
Lieut. K. Indeed I was. (*Rises, and walks restlessly to and fro.*) I never did know anything so worrying, so teasing, so perplexing in my life. (*Resumes his position.*)
Mrs. P. As I am?
Lieut. K. No, no !not you.
Mrs. P. A penny for your thoughts *now*, Kingston dear.
Lieut. K. My dear Mrs. Pontifex, I assure you they are not worth it.

Mrs. P. Now, Kingston dear, why do you call me Mrs. Pontifex? It seems very formal to a woman whom you are about to marry. When the late Col. Pontifex – *then* only Captain Pontifex – was making his addresses to me, he always called me Selina.

Lieut. K. And *I'll* call you Selina if you wish it.

Mrs. P. Now, Kingston dear, that's very kind of you – very. You're not annoyed with me for alluding to poor dear Colonel Pontifex, are you?

Lieut. K. Who? I? Oh, by no means. . . . The fact is that my head is full of my approaching interview with my father, and I was wondering how he would receive – – –[18]

The father's position with respect to his intended bride is little short of embarrassing. He finds it almost impossible to unbend and behave as a lover usually does. We shall take a glance at the Admiral.

Adm. . . . Mary, me dear! Mary!

Miss Mortimer. Coming, grandpapa.

Adm. (Coming away from door.) Psha! I wish the little baggage would leave off that silly custom of calling me grandpapa.

Enter Miss Mortimer

Miss M. Here I am, grandpapa – What do you want?

Adm. Why, my dear, in the first place, I want you to leave off calling me grandpapa, now that we are going to be man and wife.

Miss M. I'll try, but I think it will be very difficult; I have been used to it so long. You know, you taught me to call you so yourself when I was a little girl, and used to sit upon your knee.

Adm. That's very true, my dear; but that was twelve or fourteen years ago, and it was a joke. I have changed my opinion since, and now I think it's no joke.

Miss M. Well, just as you like, grand – I mean, just as you like, sir.

Adm. No, I don't like "sir" neither.

Miss M. What then?

Adm. Why, to say the truth, there *is* a little awkwardness about it. My christian name, as you know, is Theodore; but as there is *rather* more than the usual difference between our ages, perhaps that would sound a little romantic. – Suppose you call me Admiral?

Miss M. I shall like that better than anything, for I hope you don't think that I am going to marry you, because you're rich.[19]

[18] *Naval Engagements*, I, ii.
[19] *Ibid.*, I, iii.

Matters eventually, as we indicated above, are straightened out
when the son chooses Mary Mortimer as his bride-to-be and the
Admiral sees that a man of his age would be happier with Mrs.
Pontifex as a wife. We can understand the satisfaction of the
Alamo Hall audience when they saw harmony at length established in the marital status of the Admiral and his son at the end
of the play.

Lieut. K. A thought strikes me –
Adm. What is it?
Lieut. K. Do you find yourself comfortable?

[At this point, it should be stated, playwright Dance has naturally contrived to have the Admiral take Mrs. Pontifex in his
arms and the Lieutenant Mary Mortimer in his. The Lieutenant's
question would therefore seem pertinent.]

Adm. Very!
Lieut. K. So do I; then suppose we change wives, and remain as we
are.
Adm. It's all in the family, ma'am; what say you?
Mrs. Pontifex. My dear sir, I told you that the first wish of my heart
was to please your son; my next to please you. I see that his happiness
is concerned, and I consent at once.
Lieut. K. My dear Mrs. Pontifex, what *shall* I say to you?
Mrs. P. Say, "Thank you mamma," and be a good boy for the future.
Lieut. K. My Mary won't object?
Miss M. Well, I don't know that I shall.
Adm. Why, Miss Mary! what has become of your resolution to marry
an admiral? have you forgotten Duncan, Nelson, Howe and Jarvis!
Miss M. (Giving her hand to Lieut. K.) They were *all* lieutenants
once, sir.[20]

A pretty little two act play, *Naval Engagements* is, and let us
hope that Miss Carlotta and Mr. Stevens presented the ladies and
gentleman at Alamo Hall with fine assumptions of their respective
roles.

Among the notables who came from the Vaudeville to entertain
patrons at Alamo Hall were Butler and McIntyre, "acrobatic"
song and dance men; after an engagement of some weeks at both
playhouses, the two entertainers enjoyed a benefit (on March 26,

[20]   *Ibid.*, II, iii.

1875). Shortly thereafter Howard and Heath (the latter drawing at the time – the *Express* said – the "unrivalled" salary of $100 a week) came for a short stay as a song and dance team. It was in San Antonio at this time that Monroe and Heath joined forces to become one of the best known burnt-cork (or black-face) vaudeville teams in the history of the American stage.[21]

Miss Mollie Sommers, written up in the newspaper ads and on the playbills as "that unrivalled Dutch gal", must have been deserving of the praise so bestowed. Not only was she adept in her renditions of German dialect songs, but she could oblige (as she often did) by actually singing in the German tongue. "Thou are so near and yet so far", was rendered wholly in German. Another of her songs in this language was, "Die Sternlein die am Himmelszelt".

Sometimes in the presentations by the Vaudeville troupe at Alamo Hall, the olio preceded the play, and just as often the order of the day was reversed. At the end of the first week in January (1875) Tennyson's *Dora* (a dramatized version, of course) was presented; then came an olio of specialties, the whole concluding with the farce, *Our Country Cousin*. A few nights later the bill listed *Who Killed Cock Robin*; then came the olio; and, to conclude, the two-act farce of *Toodles* was offered.

The eminent nineteenth-century dramatic critic, Laurence Hutton, thought that actor William E. Burton's assumption of Toodles was the greatest laugh-provoking rendition of a comic part ever seen on the American stage.[22]

A short passage from the farce will indicate the humor of the piece.[23] In the opening scene, we find husband, Timothy, and wife, Tabatha, Toodles in a lively dialogue. As Mr. and Mrs. Toodles enter the stage, we hear the husband chiding the wife for her passion of buying things at auction.

---

[21] Edwin Le Roy Rice, *Monarchs of Minstrelsy*, p. 155.
[22] Laurence Hutton, *Plays and Players*, I, 4.
[23] William Evans Burton will be recalled as founder of the *Gentleman's Magazine*, of which Poe for a time was editor. Burton also founded and was proprietor of Burton's Theatre, New York City, in 1848. He was generally regarded as a leading comic actor in his time. James D. Hart, *Oxford Companion to American Literature*.

Mrs. Toodles. But, my dear Toodles.

Toodles. Oh, don't dear Toodles me – you'll drive me mad – your conduct is scandalous in the extreme.

Mrs. T. My dear Toodles, don't say so.

Toodles. But I will say so, Mrs. Toodles. What will become of us, with your passion of going to auctions, and buying everything you see, because it's cheap. I say, Mrs. Toodles, where's the money? and echo answers, where?

Mrs. T. I'm sure, my dear Toodles, I lay it out to the best advantage.

Toodles. . . . . I won't have my house turned into a hospital for invalid furniture. At the end of the week I ask where's the money – all gone too – spent in damned nonsense.

Mrs. T. My love, although they are of no use to you at present, we may want them, and how useful it will be to have them in the house.

Toodles. Why, Mrs. T., the house is full already of damaged chairs, and dilapidated tables, sofas with one leg, washstands with two legs, chairs with three legs, and some without a leg to stand on.

Mrs. T. I'm sure you can't find fault with the last bargain I bought.

Toodles. What is it?

Mrs. T. A pair of crutches.

Toodles. A pair of crutches? What use are they to me, Mrs. T.?

Mrs. T. No, not at present; but you might meet with an accident, and then how handy it will be to have them in the house.

Toodles. Oh, here's a woman goes to an auction and buys a pair of crutches in anticipation that her husband will break his legs. But look what you did the other day, when this railroad was finished out here, why, curse me if you did not buy forty-three wheelbarrows – some with wheels, and some without wheels. . . . The other day I saw a cart before the door, and two men carrying into the house a door-plate.

Mrs. T. My dear Toodles.

Toodles. And the name of Thompson upon it. Thompson with a P. Mrs. Toodles, if I were not innately a sober man, you would drive me to an extreme case of drinking. Well, what was your reason for buying the door-plate? "Toodles, my dear," says you, "we may have a daughter, and that daughter may be a female – and live to the age of maturity – and she *may* marry a man of the name of Thompson – with a P – then, how handy will it be to have it in the house."

Mrs. T. And won't it, dear?

Toodles. You had it stuck over the mantel-piece, and when I come down to breakfast or home to dinner, there's that odious name of Thompson looking me in the face. If I had a daughter, and caught a man of the name of Thompson making love to her, I'd break his head with that door-plate.

Mrs. T. But, my dear Toodles –
Toodles. Yes, Mrs. T., I say religiously, morally, sincerely and emphatically, damn Thompson.

As Act II is about to end, we discover Mr. Toodles, in a slightly inebriated condition, informing his wife that he, too, has been to the auction and has bought something for her.

Mrs. T. What is it – eh, dear?
Toodles. As soon as I saw it, I said to myself, it will be just the fit for my dear Tabitha!

After some hesitancy, Toodles reveals that his bargain is a coffin.

Toodles. We don't want it just now, but we don't know what will happen, and then how handy it will be to have it in the house.[24]

The *Express*, in commenting on the Alamo Hall engagements, said that, "All the ladies of the city will have the opportunity of witnessing the [Vaudeville] performances – and many gentlemen also who do not regularly attend will take their wives and children."[25]

Although somewhat lacking in aesthetic appeal, the Alamo Hall had about it an air of respectability that the Vaudeville Theatre was never able to acquire. It was here at the Alamo Hall that Thomas Alva Edison's ingenious contrivance later called the "phonograph" was introduced to San Antonians. The noteworthy event took place on November 3, 1878.

The use of the Literary Society's club rooms was often extended to the Belknap Rifles, as well as to the San Antonio Rifles, two of the city's crack military organizations. In fact, many of the Literary Society gentlemen members had their names on the rosters of the military companies.

Military societies, which had been a part of the American scene since the Revolutionary War, had long played a conspicuous rôle in the social life of San Antonio. There was, however, a dead earnestness of purpose in the armed service units of the Alamo City that would have made them unfit subjects for such humorous

---

24 "Toodles", *New York Drama*, IV, 314.
25 *Express* (February 10, 1875).

sketches as we find in Johnson Jones Hooper's *Simon Suggs of the Talapoosa Volunteers.*

"Now charge baggonets! Hooraw! Let 'em have the cold steel, my brave boys!" [26] Such a command as that uttered by Captain Suggs of the Talapoosy Voluntaires would have seemed damnably incongruous falling from the lips of any San Antonio officer of the period of which we speak. The San Antonio outfits were top-flight drill units fully capable of actual duty under arms. The oldest of these associations was the Alamo Guards. It had become an effective combat body as early as 1859; on its rolls had been such prominent citizens as Joseph E. Dwyer, Trevanion T. Teal, and Hamilton Bee; the Guards volunteered and entered the Confederate service at the outbreak of the War in 1861.

The two companies most active in the latter half of the century were the Belknap and the San Antonio Rifles. In 1886, these two service groups joined forces to quell disturbances in the border town of Laredo, to which place they had been called for that particular purpose. The Belknap Company, founded by Colonel Augustus Belknap, received its charter in 1883, and gained considerable distinction under Captain R. Green. In 1887 the two San Antonio companies won prizes "for best company drill and best individual drill" at a competition in Washington, D. C. Not long after their founding each of these bands of men-at-arms had established armories, buildings that served both as work and recreational centers; in these structures formal and informal hops were held during the year.

The rifle companies were a dominant social force in San Antonio. Some of their festive occasions, such as the one at the Berg mansion, at the corner of Acequia (later Main Avenue) and Romana Streets, were notable events in the social calendar of the city. On August 16, 1886, at the Berg home, a grand reception was held in honor of the San Antonio Rifles. The *Express* noted that the Rifles had "taken the major portion of the cake at Galveston and brought back most of the island with them". The ladies were prompt in attendance that evening and had filled the

---

[26]   Johnson Jones Hooper, "Simon Suggs Becomes Captain", *Simon Sugg's Adventures* (Philadelphia, 1881).

parlor before the gentlemen (at arms) arrived. These, however, the honorees of the evening, were not long in appearing. They "struck the front gallery two abreast. And stopped at the sharp command from their captain: 'Company, halt!' " Soon all were inside. Handsome masculine figures in uniform made an imposing sight as they mingled with beautiful ladies tastefully dressed. And the setting was consonant with such an assemblage.

At one end of the parlor of the mansion, which was pannelled in curly pine, the United States flag was draped. At the other end of the room was hung the beautiful Lone Star banner of the organization (so the *Express* reported). Under the National flag was a bank of evergreens, with the letters, "S. A. R.", in white and red roses. The event of the evening was the presentation of a gold watch to Captain F. J. Badger. This object was a handsomely engraved piece with "a split-second or time-keeper". Attached to the watch was a heavy double chain of solid gold.[27]

Young Willie Porter had an intimate enough acquaintance with military companies to know much of the mysteries of those organizations. It is likely, however, that he was more interested in the off-the-field activities of the militia units than in any competitive drills their members might have engaged in. His biographers at least give us such a sketch of the young man.[28] He was at different times a lieutenant in the Austin Grays and a corporal in the Texas Rifles of the National Guard. The heir of his invention, Willie Robbins, embodies traits of a young officer that one might aptly designate as "one of the finest"; and the story in which Robbins is presented, *"The Moment of Victory"*, is a detailed treatment of the functions and deeds of a military body from the drawing-room to the battlefield.

If Porter knew nothing about active military service from first-hand experience, it would have been easy enough for him to imagine what work under fire is like, and imagine such a condition

---

27 *Express* (August 17, 1886).
28 For an account of O. Henry's connections with militia companies, see Robert H. Davis and Arthur B. Maurice, *The Caliph of Bagdad*, Chapter III; and E. Hudson Long, *O. Henry, The Man and His Work*, Chapter IV.

he did. An author who can show us a Cisco Kid who "rubs out" his victims merely to see them kick should have little trouble giving the reader a life-like sketch of a war hero in the act of gathering laurels on the firing-line just to show a former girl-friend he could be "fly" if he wanted to.

In *"The Moment of Victory"*, the question arises, as narrators Ben Granger and "Bill" foregather in the former's general store, as to what it is that moves men to seek acclaim and renown in the market-place, on the battlefield, and elsewhere. Bill cites ambition, avarice, and the love of woman as the forces usually credited with furnishing the urge. But Ben Granger knows of a case where none of these factors was brought into play.

He tells of Willie Robbins, a townsman of his, who lacks the looks, the ease of discourse, and the grace on the dance floor it takes to cut a pleasing figure on festive occasions; he lacks these assets, yet he possesses the desire to rush in like a fool and fear to tread like an angel at all and whatever social doings were booked in the town of San Augustine. There is an ice cream sociable one evening at the home of Mrs. Colonel Spraggins. As Robbins stands before a mirror brushing his hair in the cloak room at the Spraggins' home, Myra Allison, the belle of the village, sticks her head in at the door, and asks Willie what he is doing to himself in the glass.

"I'm trying to look *fly*," says Willie.
"Well, you never could *be* fly," says Myra.

Ben Granger and Willie Robbins, as members of the San Augustine Rifles, go off to the Spanish-American War, which breaks out just after Robbins' unhappy experience with Myra Allison.

Cuba proves to be the stage for the exercise of Robbins' ambition. He seeks and finds the bubble reputation even in the cannon's mouth. He takes all sorts of chances and risks and wins all kinds of honors. After a time he is promoted to captain of his company; and San Augustine, Galveston, St. Louis, New York, and Kansas City papers "print his picture and columns of stuff about him". And for what does he make all of this grand display of bravery?

Well, we find out when he returns home following the end of the war. Reaching San Augustine by train, he drops off with Ben Granger at the depot, skips the brass-bands and the crowds that await him at the court house; and "walks out a piece" with Ben to the home Joe Granberry has built for his wife Myra Allison. Willie walks up to Myra, who sits, with her hair smoothed back and tied in a knot, on the porch. Willie looks splendid in his uniform, with his breast covered with medals and a sword with a gold haft hanging at his side.

Then he says to Myra, slowly: *"Oh, I don't know! Maybe I could if I tried!"* [29]

And it is then that we agree with Willie Robbins that he could *be* fly if he took a notion to do so.

Robbins' incentive for his deeds of derring-do is more easily understood if we take note of a romantic act that Porter himself indulged in when a member of the Texas Rifles of Austin. Porter and a fellow officer had refused to go with their company when called to Fort Worth during a railroad strike in that city. Learning later on that a girl whom he knew expected to see him with his company as the military unit passed through Waco, Porter, changing his mind about making the trip, notified the captain in Fort Worth by wire of his intention and received "transportation" for his squad. As the group passed through Waco, Porter, à la Willie Robbins, stood bolt upright on the pilot (called by some the "cow-catcher") of the locomotive pulling the troop train. The girl relates that she got a view of him and he one of her. And the mere sight of her was apparently satisfaction enough to him for making the journey.[30]

---

[29] Italics and punctuation are O. Henry's: "The Moment of Victory", *Works*, I, 763.
[30] Arthur W. Page, "Little Pictures of O. Henry", *The Bookman*, 1913.

III

TURNER HALL

It is not likely that any of the Turners at the time of the establishment of their athletic society had foresight enough to envision the important rôle their club house was to play in the cultural life of San Antonio. This German fraternal organization, the Turnverein, in 1879 removed from their quarters on Alamo Plaza to a site on the south side of West Houston Street near the intersection of St. Mary's. At this place, the Society built an attractive structure of two stories in height, with an auditorium and recreation rooms, accommodations considered ample for all purposes at the time of the erection. By the summer of 1882, however, it was found necessary to alter and improve the building, then well known in the city as Turner Hall. The stage in the auditorium was refitted and eight new dressing-rooms were constructed in a conveniently adjacent area. These additions were considered satisfactory to the demands of the entertainers who regularly graced the "boards" of the Hall. Not unmindful of the needs of the Turners themselves, the directors had a dining-room made back of the stage, as well as an amply arranged recreation hall, with an adjoining ten-pin alley. The auditorium of Turner Hall had for a number of years served as the leading theatre of San Antonio. The use of the club building as a playhouse would seem to have been quite as much an aim of the planners of the building as its employment for recreational purposes.

Because of the importance of the theatre in American social life in that era, Turner Hall became a focal point of the cultural life of the Alamo City. The structure still held its place with undiminished lustre in 1882, a significant year in the life of William Sydney Porter.

The theatre of the eighties in large measure portrayed the life and reflected the tastes of the people on whom it depended for support. And of course life, as well as the tastes of the people, was then as now infinitely various. And while producers generally must have tried to satisfy the preferences of the playgoers, some, we may presume, made efforts to remold the tastes of theatre patrons. The San Antonio *Light*, quoting the New Orleans *Times-Democrat* of September 9, 1882, gives an idea of how theatrical producers tried to cater to the wishes of playgoers throughout the nation. The New Orleans journal prefaced its remarks with the observation that the two-hundred odd theatres in the country had got rid of their stock companies and would depend on travelling troupes to fulfill a function that in previous years had been in a measure the concern of "provincial" managers. The paper then went on to say that it figured that about one-third of the two hundred and fifty travelling companies would be "shipwrecked" during the season. (We recall in this connection a remark in O. Henry's "Strictly Business" that seems aptly to fit the situation: "All shows walk back to New York on tan oxford and railroad ties." [1]

The *Times-Democrat* article said:

Of these new travelling companies, one-hundred-thirty-six are devoted to legitimate drama; twenty-seven to comedy; forty to opera; twenty-four to minstrelsy; seventeen to the spectacular; eleven to legerdermain, and such like. The opera companies are stronger than before and the whole country will be flooded with *Patience, Billie Taylor,* and *Mascot* troupes. Farce and burlesque companies would be fewer; and there are no less than four *Hazel Kirke* companies on the road.

The article concluded with the statement that the dramatic world had not improved – in fact, it was in a rut – and that the offerings of the year were demoralizing to American talent.

An American comedian who seldom missed a year in visiting Texas was Sol Smith Russell. There is reason to suppose that O. Henry may have found interest in Russell's assumption of Tom Dilloway. The actor introduced the character to San Antonio in

[1] O. Henry, *Works*, II, 1484.

J. E. Brown's homespun comedy, *Edgewood Folks*, at Turner
Hall on Nov. 3, 1882. An *Express* critic said of Russell: "A
speaking countenance, combined with inimitable powers of mim-
icry and intelligent conception of the requisites of his created
rôle, leaves nothing further to be said in commendation." And of
Fred E. Bond, in the part of Ferguson, a tramp, the same writer
declared that he "was so natural in make-up and acting that
housekeepers will double-lock their doors during the remainder
of the engagement". A *Light* reporter found one scene of the
play worthy of Hogarth; it was that in which Bond's Ferguson
and Russell's Tom Dilloway held drunken orgies. Mr. Russell's
facial expressions alone frequently "left the audience convulsed
with laughter".

At the Russell performances downstairs seats were at a pre-
mium and standing room in the galleries "way above par".

Russell was to establish a national reputation with this play
after four more years of presenting his Tom Dilloway throughout
the country. The actor excelled in portraying odd types of American characters, "uncouth in physique, unschooled in social conventionalities, but with minds alert, ... and with the ... never-say-
die spirit".[2]

O. Henry excelled in his portrayal of uncouth characters, often
unschooled in social conventionalities, but did not seem to be
particularly strong on emphasizing the never-say-die spirit – if
the latter smacked of moral teaching. "A story with a moral ... is
like the bill of a mosquito", he says in "The Gold that Glittered".
"It bores you, and then injects a stinging drop to irritate your
conscience." But of the unconventional characters he presents in
the Southwest stories, ones that may have reminded theatre-goers
of Russell's impersonations, we like to recall Mack Lonsbury,
who sits in his stocking-feet and reads Buckle's *History of Civilization*;[3] Paisley Fish and his friend Telemachus Hicks, rivals in
the strange courtship of the widow Jessup;[4] the persistent and
undaunted Lucullus Polk, who hopes to sell his turquoise-studded

---

[2]   Lewis G. Strang, *Famous Actors of the Day in America*, p. 249.
[3]   "The Ransom of Mack", *Works*, I, 118.
[4]   "Telemachus, Friend", *ibid.*, I, 123.

saddle to the Iman of Muskat;[5] Caligula Polk (enough like Lucullus to be a cousin), who, absent-minded, with the *rurales* chasing him, swims the Rio Grande with a brick in each hand;[6] and Sam Galloway, troubadour and avenger, who rides a pony with a Dante Alighieri face.[7]

It was not by accident that O. Henry hit upon the phrase, "Strictly Business", as a title for one of his books, as well as for the designation of the lead story of the collection itself. "Strictly Business" was a popular expression typical of the boom times of the eighties and nineties. Unbridled speculation was rife in this post-Civil War period. Mark Twain, who could see little humor in the get-rich-quick schemes of Beriah Sellars, was certainly not free himself of this urge to amass wealth at all hazards. "Literature, even after his early great successes, was to him merely a money-making affair."[8] Money was just as much a passion with him as it was with Balzac. Twain's *The Gilded Age* was of course written on the speculation theme; and A. C. Gunther's farce, bearing the designation, *Strictly Business*, was one of the many dramas that playfully satirized that age of acquisitiveness. Gunther's farce was first presented in San Antonio on October 24, 1882. C. B. Bishop, a highly talented comedian, who had made a fine Pistol in *Henry V* a few years before, and who later was to make a great success in the rôle of the Widow Bedott, delighted a large audience with his portrayal of Phineas Pomeroy Philkins, the main character of the Gunther play. Bishop's Philkins was a "breezy and cheeky" American canned goods salesman trying to vend his wares in Russia. His mishaps and adventures in the land of the Czar furnish the humor of the piece. But Philkins, like Beriah Sellars, is out to make money; the acquisition of specie is his prime objective.

Winona Cherry, in the initial story of O. Henry's more extensive work under the same title as Gunther's farce, tells Bob Hart that she is "strictly business". Hart had just asked her if she

---

5   "Seats of the Haughty", *ibid.*, I, 144.
6   "Hostages to Momus", *ibid.*, I, 337.
7   See Chapter XII, Note 19.
8   Fred Lewis Pattee, *Mark Twain*, xxx.

would be his partner in the production of a vaudeville sketch he had written. "I'm on the stage for what it pays me", the girl explains. It develops that Hart is governed by a similar philosophy. Miss Cherry likes Hart's proposal so well that the two join forces in the successful production of Hart's sketch, called *Mice Will Play.*

If a person were looking for motifs, he could truthfully say that *Mice Will Play* is on the acquisitiveness theme. There can be little doubt about that fact, for Old "Arapahoe" Grimes, the quarter-million-dollar cattle king in the sketch, dies on the same day he receives $647,000 in cash for a drove of beeves he sells in the East. But in the story itself ("Strictly Business", of *Strictly Business*) Winona Cherry and Bob Hart are depicted as very modest in their notions of affluence; at the time Winona accidentally shoots Bob in the neck (a miscue in the business of the sketch), the latter is reported to have his bungalow almost paid for and Winona herself has "so many savings deposit bank-books that she had begun to buy sectional book-cases on the installment plan to hold them". Also at this point in the story it is revealed that Bob and Winona have been married for two years. Thus we might construe that Cherry and Hart have an aim in life other than the acquisition of material wealth.

In the persons of the ambitious but quiet, hard-working vaudeville team the author neatly satirizes the money-making urge of the era by showing that the reasonable wishes of a couple of poor players are more apt to bring happiness than the unrestrained desires of the speculator.

William Sydney Porter, in his concept of the solid virtues of life, must have been pretty much like his Bob Hart. We can imagine him as being quite as well pleased in his room at the Caledonia in New York or in a bungalow in Austin as Mark Twain was in his pretentious Hartford mansion or taking his ease in a carved Florentine bed.[9]

Ever since the appearance of Thomas Rowlandson's plates (1819), made to illustrate William Combe's *Dr. Syntax in Search*

[9]   For the best account of W. S. Porter as a practitioner of the doctrine of acquisitiveness, see Gerald Langford, *Alias O. Henry*, V, VI, VII.

Empire Theatre (formerly Turner Opera House).

of the Picturescue, the schoolmaster has been an object of light ridicule by writers and painters. It can also be said that since Dr. Syntax's first appearance in print, the grotesque schoolmaster and his descendants have proved a lucrative source of amusement for the theatrical producer.

On March 5, 1881, at Daly's Theatre in New York, Woolson Morse's musical paraphrase, *Cinderella at School*, was seen for the first time on any stage. The presentation was under the personal direction of Augustin Daly, and although the playwright was careful to explain that his drama "was paraphrased" from the German musical piece *Aschenbrodel*, *Cinderella* bears a noticeable resemblance to T. W. Robertson's natural comedy, "School".[10]

In the Morse musical, Miss Zenobia Tropics, "a firm believer in bone-forming", is head teacher of the Papyrus Seminary. Her principal is Professor Kindergarten, a mild-mannered, inoffensive person, who is almost of no consequence. Professor Syntax, Kindergarten's head usher and chief "husher", a fantastic, hypocritical creature something on the order of Malvolio, shares honors with Miss Tropics as the main source of merriment in the farce.

Arthur Bicycle, "a perambulating Deity of the Upper Crust", and his friend, Jack Polo, "of the Meadow Brook Hunt", are lovers in what could be called the main plot. Bicycle falls in love with and finally marries Niobe Marsh, a charity pupil of talent, who proves in the end to be the long lost daughter of Lord Lawntennys' brother. Lord Lawntennys, uncle to Bicycle, has come to America from England in search of his niece. Polo marries one of the pupils, a rich girl from Brazil, named Merope Mallow, who is sketched as "comparatively ignorant, but superlatively 'smart' ".

Other schoolgirls have such names as Chloris Slatepencil, who lisps; Circe Slatepencil, who giggles; Pansy Pickle, who knows everything; Primrose Pickle who knows nothing; Sally Chalk, who pouts; and Daisy Dimple, a simple little thing.

There are seven songs in the comedy, including "Green are the Waving Trees", and "Now Poor Cinderella"; but the humor

10   Joseph Francis Daly, *The Life of Augustin Daly*, XXI, 341-343.

of the piece is derived mainly from Zenobia Tropics' attempt to instruct the pupils and Syntax's absurdities. An additional source of mirth is furnished by the girls in the choruses: Chloris Slate-pencil lisps her part; Circe mingles her words with giggles; Lotis accompanies her song with sighs; and Penelope eats as she sings.

On the whole, *Cinderella at School* subjects the various phases of life in and about Papyrus Seminary to a mild and searching banter.

Joseph Francis Daly found praise for Mrs. G. H. Gilbert's portrayal of Zenobia Tropics and James Lewis's Dr. Syntax in the initial performance of *Cinderella*. Mrs. Gilbert, as head-teacher in the Seminary, Daly said, disciplined her scholars with an Amazonian firmness and a terpsichorean grace that was matchless in execution. Lewis, he added, rendered Dr. Syntax with such a degree of naturalness that the auditor felt that the player had stepped out of a Rowlandson drawing. The drama was such a good piece of fun that it played for sixty-five nights, despite the severe criticism directed at Woolson Morse's attempt at musical composition.[11]

A year after *Cinderella at School* first graced the boards at Daly's New York Theatre, Henry E. Dixey introduced the farce to San Antonians. Dixey visited the city as leading light of E. E. Rice's "Surprise Party". In this play which had been a Daly hit the year before, Dixey appeared as Dr. Syntax (a part which the San Antonio *Light* declared he cleverly portrayed); and George K. Fortescue, incomparable burlesque artist (an individual who regularly tipped the beam at three-hundred-seventy-five pounds), kept the whole house convulsed with laughter, as Miss Zenobia Tropics. The antics and contortions of this gigantean mimicker as he instructed his charges in the art of the dance "evoked prodigious enthusiasm". It is fairly reasonable to conjecture that Mr. Fortescue acquitted himself as handsomely in this part as had Mrs. Gilbert the year before.

The success of *Cinderella* must have given the idea of a school travesty to other producers. One of those so inspired was John

[11]   *Ibid.*

Ince, father of the better known Thomas Ince of later movie fame. Ince concocted and produced (and continued to produce for a number of years) a "slap-bang" farce which he called *Fun in a Boarding School*. Although this hotchpotch of gags and clever lines can be thought of as one of the many "fun" farces (as for instance, *Fun in the Police Court, Fun in a Hotel, Fun at Coney Island, Fun in the Kitchen*), there is more evidence to support the belief that the piece is in the "school" tradition. Ince himself was cast in the major rôle of the offering, as Professor Jeremiah Gimcracks, F. R. S., L. L. D., N. G., D. D. During the mid-November engagement at Turner Hall in 1882, the bright spot of Ince's performance was his rendering of Sergeant Buzzfuzz's speech from *Pickwick Papers*. It was not the Buzzfuzz speech, however, that drew commendation from the press writers. The song and dance act of Lisetta Illani took up the space in their columns. The *Light* did indicate that the humor of the farce centered in Professor Gimcrack's efforts to bring order out of the chaos of the classroom. But since most of the professor's scholars seemed dead-bent on tripping a fantastic toe rather than delving into the mysteries of syntax, it can be deduced that the old bird had a rough time of it. Professor Gimcrack is prevented by the appearance of the prompter from having to put up with either "turn out" or triumph. This functionary comes finally to say that it is time to end the revels by a well-executed song and dance.[12]

Few in the audience at Turner Hall in November of 1882 could have known that A. B. Longstreet ever told of an old frontier custom of schoolboys "turning the master out" so they could have a holiday;[13] it is more likely that some may have been familiar with another "turn out" in Edward Eggleston's *Hoosier Schoolmaster*;[14] and certainly many who witnessed *Fun in a Boarding School* knew the portrait that Dickens gives us of Wackford Squeers of Dotheboys Hall. "B-o-t, bot, t-i-n, bottin, n-e-y, ney, bottiney, noun substantive, . . . That's our system, Nickleby; what

12   San Antonio *Light* (November 16, 1882).
13   A. B. Longstreet, "The Turn Out", *Georgia Scenes*, p. 62.
14   Edward Eggleston, *The Hoosier Schoolmaster*, Chapter XIII.

do you think of it?" [15] Mr. Squeers graces the pages of *Nicholas Nickleby*. Nor should we overlook the possibility that a scant few of the auditory may have made acquaintance with Bret Harte's Eudoxia Tish, one of "the two old cats" who have Colonel Starbottle's ward, Pansy Stannard, under their governance. Pansy, we recall, is delighted at the impression her guardian makes on her two teachers: "Frightened 'em! – the two old cats! Frightened 'em outen their slippers! Oh, *never, never* before was they so skeert!" [16]

One of those who must certainly have known of both Wackford Squeers and Eudoxia Tish was William Sydney Porter. It is much more likely, however, that this young newcomer to southwest Texas would be more deeply impressed with Fortescue's assumption of Zenobia Tropics, or Henry Dixey's Dr. Syntax. Dr. Syntax and Miss Tropics strike us as being the kind of instructors that would have interested the two-hundred and nineteen huskies that Peters and Tucker gather in Floresville.

O. Henry writes his playful satire of college life, "The Chair of Philanthromathematics", as a story of *The Gentle Grafter* series. The actors in this humorous drama of Arizona college life are the inimitable pair of opportunists, or "beats", Jeff Peters and Andy Tucker. Andy is a kind of grown-up Tom Sawyer, who can always conjure up something to do when he thinks an occasion demands that something. Peters and Tucker remind one in a way of Twain's Duke and King, with a generous admixture of modified elements of the character of Simon Suggs.[17] The two O. Henry creations are fine-edged sharpers, who, although they "get tuck" once in a while, the reader finds it difficult to imagine them as being unwary enough ever to become the victims of Dr. Tar and Professor Feather, as the King and Duke do. Liken Peters and Tucker to Simon Suggs and recall how Suggs takes a fling at the faro "tiger" at Clare's gambling saloon in Tuskaloosa. He's badly whipped by the tiger, but his "mother wit" enables him to leave

---

[15] Charles Dickens, *The Life and Adventures of Nicholas Nickleby*, Chapter VIII.
[16] "A Ward of Colonel Starbottle", *The Writings of Bret Harte*, XIX, 121.
[17] Johnson Jones Hooper, "The Captain Attends a Camp-Meeting", *op. cit.*. XLVII, 425.

Clare's with $200 furnished him by his "nephy" Jeemes Peyton. On top of that, as Jeemes' phony uncle he has the satisfaction of setting up the house to a $63 champagne and oyster supper with said "nephy" Jeemes unwittingly standing the treat.[18] And Twain's King is not a whit more shifty than Suggs when the Captain mulcts the camp-meeting worshippers out of nigh a hundred dollars and goes with their blessing over to the "krick-swamp" to pray over the ill-gotten sum.[19]

Since we know that Peters and Tucker are business tycoons and not men of cloistered solitudes we are not surprised to find them stressing the economic aspect of their venture into the field of scholarship. Many towns, as we know, appear to want colleges established in their midst simply because of the good they will do for the town's economy. O. Henry would seem to be poking fun at this shallow idea. Peters and Tucker help business in Floresville: "A new shooting gallery and a pawnshop and two more saloons started." How well Andy contributes to the intellectual climate of the community with his lecture on "Modern Music and Prehistoric Literature of the Archipelagos" is left for the reader to guess. The only time we hear of the professors even getting in touch with the students is when we are told that they disarm the students and herd them into classes. Students of such manifest eagerness, however, we feel would be worthy recepticles in a class-room; and feeling so we wonder what luck a 375-pound female professor would have teaching such charges the fine art of dancing. These scholarly huskies would very likely drive Dr. Syntax to the brush; and Dr. Gimcracks would have to do better than try to hold them with a reading of Sergeant Buzzfuzz's speech. Gimcrack's creator himself could think of no better way to get rid of the child of his fancy than to ring the curtain down on him.

"The Chair of Philanthromathematics" is plainly in the *Fun in a Boarding School* Tradition. The students as well as the pro-

[18] Johnson Jones Hooper, "Simon Fights 'The Tiger' and Gets Whipped", *op. cit.*
[19] Johnson Jones Hooper, "The Captain Attends a Camp-Meeting", *op. cit.*

prietors derive a kind of unbounded pleasure in the "groves of
academe"; the yell they get up, at any rate, indicates as much:

> Raw, raw, raw,
> Done, done, done,
> Peters, Tucker,
> Lots of fun.

We are sorry that we do not hear Andy dispensing wisdom from
the rostrum; a man capable of the phrase, "As quiet as the campus
of a correspondence school at midnight" could leave us some
notable *bon mots* to chew on. Wisdom of Andy's oort at the
lectern somehow strikes us as fitting very well into a business
administration lecture; it is consonant with the theme of the
story: "Philanthropy when practiced in a business way is an art
that blesses him who gives as well as him who receives."

The "shiftiness" of Tucker is well illustrated when he discovers that the $25,000 with which he and his partner start their
venture has dwindled to $821.62. Tucker wires to Frisco for a
faro banker who comes to Floresville and opens shop in rooms
over the Red Front livery-stable. James Darnley McCorkle is the
educator's name and Peters is led to believe that he is a math
"prof." drawing $5000 a year. Of course the students, devoted
as they are to extra-curricular activities, flock to Professor Mc-
Corkle's classes. The denouement is the revelation that Mc-
Corkle's energy has netted the two promotors $31,000 a piece.
Jeff, who had kicked violently about the math "prof." drawing
such a high salary, is greatly pleased at the hoax. He and Andy
Tucker end their spell of fun and quit the scene with a handsome
profit from their excursion into philanthropy. The students, we
may presume, are much wiser than they were before their little
session of off-campus frivolity at World's University.

In representing Peters and Tucker and their students as ma-
terialists more responsive to the commercial factors and influences
of college life than to the scholarly, O. Henry was reflecting a
condition prevalent on some of the major American university
campuses at the time about which he writes. In June, 1905,
Henry Beach Needam began a series of articles in *McClure's
Magazine* to reveal a distressing state of affairs prevalent in col-

lege circles of the East. Many students at these institutions, Mr. Needam shows, selected the college that would best reward them for their prowess on the football field. Princeton, Yale, and Pennsylvania were more prominent among the colleges that catered to the wishes of students tainted with commercialism. In some instances eligibility standards were violated by these three schools. Charles E. Patterson, the "oldest living undergraduate of Princeton" in 1901, with an honorary degree of Master of Arts from that institution, openly recruited students of athletic bent at the "prep" schools of Exeter and Andover. An Andover athlete when questioned about his chances of passing an examination given him by Patterson made this statement:

". . . I put on my A sweater and walked in front of my proctor several times. At the top of my paper I wrote my weight – 205 pounds. I guess I'll pass all right. Patterson said I would."

"As a matter of fact", writes Needam, "he did pass; but he went to Yale."

Professor Hollis, who for seven years was chairman of the Harvard Athletic Committee, summarized his ideas of the situation.

The evils of college athletics are the evils of everyday life. Commercialism is a characteristic of American life. Sad to say, the boy goes to school and college tainted with it. He gets it at home. The teaching of American homes is primarily responsible.[20]

Commercialism, a phase of acquisitiveness, then, was a way of life in America some sixty-odd years since. In our age of affluence the taint no longer corrupts. The boys at Peters and Tucker's University were as normal in their time as beatniks and hippies are in ours.

It is no wonder that O. Henry writes playfully of Andrew Carnegie in "*The Chair of Philanthromathematics*".

So he puts up eighty million dollars' worth of libraries and the boys with the dinner pail that builds 'em get the benefit.
"Where's the books?" asks the reading public.

[20]   Henry Beach Needham, "The College Athlete, Recruiting and Subsidizing", *Mc Clure's Magazine*, XXV, No. 2 (June, 1905).

"I dinna ken," says B. "I offered ye libraries; and there they are.
. . . Hoot, for ye!"

And if the Harvard professor's words fit the inhabitants of the
realm as well as he indicates, we do not wonder at the number
of muck-raking articles appearing in *Mc Clure's* in the early years
of the present century. The journal announced in an "ad" that
Lincoln Steffens "has interrupted his series on political corruption to study *Equitable Life, A Business Graft.* It will let us see
how typical Equitable's practices are of life insurance – a subject
that touches every one of us – and how typical such practices are
of big business generally." Ida M. Tarbell would show what a
struggle the state of Kansas had to obtain a fair deal from the
rapacious Standard Oil.[21] All of this was in the October, 1905
issue.

In November, Ray Stannard Baker was to do his best to show,
in his article, *The Railroad Rate,* that "Railroad Favoritism is the
chief cause of the Trust; i.e., the oil, coal, and beef trusts." [22]

In the light of our knowledge of campus conduct at Eastern
colleges in the early nineteen-hundreds, it is not illogical to conclude that Jeff Peters and Andy Tucker might have made a "go"
of it at World's University had their academic horizon been
broader. But they appeared to be a bit short-sighted in their com-
prehension of the needs in the scholarly disciplines of a seminary
of learning.

---

[21] *Mc Clure's Magazine,* XXX, No. 5 (October, 1905).
[22] Ray Stannard Baker, "The Railroad Rate", *Mc Clure's Magazine,* XXVI,
No. 1 (November, 1905).

IV

BLOOD AND THUNDER, OFF STAGE AND ON

It is worthwhile to note that O. Henry's Southwest stories are not strictly on the "western order". Regardless of how one would classify these compositions (and this appraiser places them among the author's best creations), the stories lack an atmosphere of spilt blood and burnt powder. A tabulation of the instances of gunplay in a representative number of the stories shows that the author makes sparing use of the burnt powder factor in advancing the fortunes of his principals, whether they be peace-officers or outlaws. In "Hearts and Crosses", Webb Yeager's "girded revolvers" are integral parts of his accoutrement, as is also the Winchester rifle he carries in his saddle scabbard. These articles "belong", just as the plumed hat befits the Cavalier, and the closely cropped head of hair the Puritan. It can be noted with interest that Yeager, the owner of the armament mentioned, fires neither of the pieces during the course of the story. In "The Sphinx Apple", no firearms of any sort are even mentioned; nor do guns of any kind play a part in either "The Ransom of Mack", or "Telemachus, Friend". If any of these western critters so much as carries a side-arm, the reader is not apprised of the fact. Sanderson Pratt and Idaho Green ("The Handbook of Hymen") find a peaceful way to settle their difficulties; Judson Odom ("The Pimienta Pancakes") first uses his six-shooter to pound an antelope steak, and later to pop over a roadrunner and a rabbit-hawk, two instances of marksmanship that would certainly qualify him as a hunter of the more astute, non-feathery kind of quarry. Uncle Emsley Telfair, an accessory obstacle to the attainment of Jud's objective, makes a pass or two at his forty-five, but never quite succeeds in bringing the arm into play. In neither "Seats of the Haughty" nor "Hygeia at the Solito" are handguns brought "into requisition". Almost any western story addict would say that Cricket McGuire needs killing in half a dozen different places. The three shots fired down the river by the "masquerootin" Leandro García ("An Afternoon Miracle") are "off-stage" discharges. Bud Dawson, proprietor of the Top Notch Saloon, regards one of the shots of such little moment that he virtually ignores the wound it inflicts in his shoulder; Bob Buckley, protagonist of this story of the miracle, with his problem of fear, discards his Winchester, and later his sixes (when he discovers that García has forgotten his) and tangles with the knifebearing Mexican bandit with only his bare fists. If Bob had found an old chair or table-leg lying about somewhere near he could have leapt right into the "western-movie" tradition by beating García over the *cabeza* with one or both of the extraneous objects. The ranger's Saxon knockout blow may have established a tradition among writers in the Western vein. TV and pulp-western authors occasionally vary this mortality theme by having their hero beat the villain into a state of non-truculence with a bedrail. Of course writers of the modern script don't make use of the furniture until their hero and villain have exchanged a hundred or so rounds with their musical pistols. "The Missing Chord", definitely western in atmosphere, is as serene and shotless as a Greek pastoral. In "A Call Loan", Tom Merwin (*à la* Richard Harding Davis), with a gun in each hand, starts out to hold up a train, but Bill Longley soon shows him that such behavior is foolish. "The Princess and the Puma" offers Josefa O'Donnell with her silver-mounted .38 handgun in the astonishing feat of shooting a Mexican lion to death in mid-air. This shot is not much of a strain on our credulity, as both Josefa and Rip Givens, her lover, seem to know; so they both tease our fancy with little deceits (as lovers will), just to knock out an obstacle or so in the course of true love, if for no other purpose. We really wouldn't have expected Dry Valley Johnson ("The Indian Summer of Dry Valley Johnson") to use a more formidable weapon than a black-snake whip to force his attentions on his future bride, although Kitty Leroy in real life demonstrated the possibilities of a shotgun for a like aim. We are told that the youngest kid in Yellowhammer ("Christmas by Injunction") packs a .45 and a safety-razor. Bobby, the main kid in the story, wants a real rifle for Christmas, for reasons that most fathers can understand. The philanthropically-minded Cherokee, father-like, satisfies the kid's wishes, a very natural procedure. Armed knights capture an ogre's castle and rob a train in "A Chaparral Prince", but if e'er a gun is fired in the process of either of the two actions the reader is kept in ignorance of the indiscretion. In "The Reformation of Calliope", of course, by the very nature of the piece, an infinity of shots is fired. Calliope Catesby of the brassy steam-piano yell, sets out to tree the town of Quicksand; Buck Patterson and his deputies, tired of Catesby's foolishness after so long a time, are determined to corral the noisy roarer. Marshal Patterson, who is knocked out by concussion, and Colonel Swazey's yellow dog are the only living things who get hurt in the course of the narrative.

The "three doses" which Sam Galloway administers to King James ("The Last of the Troubadours") plainly constitute an instance of justifiable homicide, and for that reason shall be acclaimed as highly suitable to the action of which they are a part. There is quite a bit of florid gun-play as Sebastiano Saldar and his gang pull a surprise attack on the Rangers in "Jimmy Hayes and Muriel", but this is a ranger-cattle-thief story where such things fittingly occur; we must note, however, that no one is hurt in that particular scuffle, a fact noteworthy enough in itself. The fracas in which the earthly career of rookie Jimmy Hayes is brought to an end and in which he plays a hero's part, is another off-stage demonstration, presented to the reader as if the author had the decorum of a Greek tragedy in mind. If Sam Durkee ("A Technical Error") pumps six bullets with his Colt automatic "into the body the brown dress covered", a number in excess of what is needed, some will say, it should be remembered that Sam is honor-bound to uphold the Durkee end of the Durkee-Tatum feud. Feuds as a rule end in violence. Does not Mark Twain end the thirty-some-odd-year-old Harney-Shepardson feud with an outburst of carnage that wipes out the entire male contingent of the Shepardsons? And the sweetest love story ever told is built round a feud that brings the fairest members of the Montague and Capulet families to a tragic end. There is nothing particularly reprehensible about Sam's six shots. The magazine capacity of the Durkee auto was probably six cartridges, with one in the barrel. For safety's sake Sam more than likely carried the weapon with the barrel unloaded. Besides these considerations, Sam Durkee would have had ample justification to "rub out" the Tatum boy from pure unmodified revenge; Tatum had done him dirt enough to warrant such action.

In another story involving the disguise of the victim ("The Caballero's Way"), Ranger Lieutenant Sandridge (through error, of course) discharges five shots with his Winchester into the body of Tonia. In this killing, revenge is again the impelling force. A law-officer dealing with the Cisco Kid positively could not be too sure; for are we not told in the beginning of the story that the Kid had killed six men, more or less fairly, had murdered twice as many, and had murdered or killed others whom he "modestly forebore to count?" With respect to the unities, we may presume, the reader is spared accounts of these rencontres that built up the Kid's reputation.

Some readers might think it rather surprising that a story, "A Poor Rule", which has as one of its chief characters cowpoke Bud Cunningham, would contain no mention whatever of a firearm. The author-narrator sketches Bud as "the only cowboy off the stage that I ever saw who looked like one on it". To a reading public who had seen Mr. James H. Wallick in many of his blood and thunder western melodramas, an unarmed cowpoke would seem as unacceptable as the giraffe did to the country bumpkin. (We shall have more to say of James H. Wallick later on.) It is not surprising at all that no shots are fired to destroy the serenity of the scene in either "The Missing Chord", or "The Sphinx Apple". The nature of the theme in these two pieces simply does not warrant the introduction of such discord to mar their harmony. And one might apply these words just as cogently to "Cupid a la Carte"; but in the case of "The Higher Abdication" a less skillful writer than O. Henry might have let his characters get away from him. At least twice, Curly, a Truesdell as he really is, could very easily have his feuding proclivity stirred up; and goodness knows what a feudist by inheritance might do when inordinately aroused. In this last story we have another of those good old Saxon fist-fights, a bout of "strength and awkwardness" that strikes the rational reader as a "cussed sight" more acceptable as the natural behavior of man than a joust with chairs or bedrails.

The ostensibly formidable desperado Black Eagle, or Piggy, otherwise known as Chicken Ruggles ("The Passing of Black Eagle") is not constitutionally equipped to act the rôle he would essay as bandit leader. It is a tribute to his creator that he could place Chicken in the midst of a band of desperate men and represent him as gaining the respect of the rank and file of the gang (Bud King, of course, excepted), even for a short spell, and do so while utterly lacking the fierce qualities conventionally attributed to a bandit chief. The story of Black Eagle and that centered in the scheming of Black Bill ("The Hiding of Black Bill") reveal an artistry in the presentation of solid values which is seldom achieved by the writer of pure melodrama. Both of these stories of the Southwest are so artfully contrived that gunplay would be out of place in their actions.

If there must be shooting perforce (as there seems to be a need of in "One Dollar's Worth"), how distinctly individual a matter it is to have the hero Littlefield, district attorney, curtail of his life-portion a murderous, vengeful Mexican bandit, with a counterfeit dollar he had thoughtlessly left in his pocket. The use of the "phony" dollar, evidence in another case, lessens the tension as well on a secondary phase of the story-fabric. Of course Littlefield accomplishes the feat of stopping Sam with the aid of a shotgun, an act which does not in any way reflect on the originality of the conception. Nancy Derwent, the district attorney's fiancée, shielded by tall grass and a buckboard, has the pleasure of seeing her lover hero put the quietus on Mexican Sam with a slug made from a lead dollar. Such a method of removing evil as an obstacle in order to effect one's ends is certainly a notable variation on the theme of self-defence or justifiable homicide.[1]

The Llano Kid seems to be on the verge of reforming when he commits the indiscretion that results in the death of the high-born youth from the Coralitos. Maybe he would not have shot if the impetuous juvenile had not brought his gun into play first. The reader of this story, "A Double-Dyed Deceiver", is left to wonder if the young fellow wanted merely to cut an underbit in the Kid's right ear, or if he had a more deadly objective. Even if the boy intended only to mark the Kid, we cannot blame the latter too much for his retaliatory action; nobody especially relishes the idea of having his right ear shot at by a large-bore side arm. The deafening concussion, for one thing, would be an annoyance. The shooting in this story is a likely enough circumstance, and could have happened just as easily on the border anywhere, or in a more effete community.

We shall conclude our disquisition on the deliberate discharge of firearms by Western malcontents by saying a word or two about Shark Dodson and his robber associate, Bob Tidball. These two men figure in "The Roads We Take". Aside from the fact that the story seems to have been concocted mainly as a dream to illustrate the callousness of a Wall Street broker, the rude display of firearms that the reader observes in the reverie-portion is not too much to expect when a money-baron is daydreaming of train robbery. Besides, by way of a mitigating circumstance, Bob Tidball, instead of merely knocking an idea out of the express messenger's head with the butt-end of his revolver, could just as easily have spilled his brains with a close-range shot. By this exercise of restraint, the reader is spared an effusion of blood that he might have found shocking to his tastes. And, supposing that Bob had elected to fire, it is hardly probable that the mes-

---

[1] McDaniels, a highwayman, who had escaped from a San Antonio jail on May 14, 1885, wrote a threatening letter to the San Antonio *Daily Express* on June 19. O. Henry, as the reader may recall, uses this business of the threatening letter when he has Mexico Sam write one to the judge in "One Dollar's Worth". McDaniels came to grief a few weeks after he had written his letter (July 1) when United States marshals Van Riper and Stevens ended his earthly career at a goat camp near Boerne, Texas. (William Corner, *op. cit.*, p. 148.)

senger minutes later could have given the Creek chevalier of industry, John Big Dog, his just due as an accessory villain. Big Dog's exit is decorous enough. We do recoil somewhat later at the dastardly behavior of Dodson towards his pal of three years. Looked at from one point of view, however, Shark's act can be excused as a matter of expediency; it is by this time pretty clear to the discriminating reader that Bolivar cannot carry double. Such a reader is further relieved of the shock of the murder when he finds that it has implications of greater import than those first presented.

V

COWS AND HORSES

One might mention as illustrative of the "muscular" western variety a dozen stories besides those just considered; but the ones listed are enough to emphasize the point that although William Sydney Porter may have witnessed *The Bandit King* and *The Cattle King* on any of several occasions when actor James H. Wallick brought these two burnt powder and cold steel melodramas to Turner Hall in the eighties, the later O. Henry did not patently reflect a knowledge of the tradition established by this depicter of border-life realism and romance.

In writing of Wallick's performance of *The Bandit King* at Turner Hall in October of 1884, an *Express* reviewer spoke of the piece as "a tolerably well toned down border drama with all the excitement and thrilling scenes and the coarseness completely eliminated". Wallick's fine physique and powerful voice, in the journal's estimate, seemed to atone for the excessive discharge of firearms. Two fine-looking horses, "Roan Charger", and "Bay Rider", may also have been factors in arousing enthusiasm in the large audience that saw Wallick's two plays. Theatre patrons since the days of *Mazeppa* had found great pleasure at the sight of prancing horses on the stage.[1]

As Bob Taylor, the hero of *The Cattle King*, companion piece to *The Bandit King*, Wallick marries his heroine on horseback. The conjugal act was considered the big moment of the melo-

---

[1] The most popular of several dramas based on Byron's poem *Mazeppa* was by the English playwright H. M. Milner. The drama featured a harzardous ride up a mountain path by Mazeppa, who was tied face upward on the back of a wild horse of Tartary.

drama; a lurid polychrome of giant dimensions on the box-car (or rather palace stock-car) that carried Wallick's horses from town to town depicted the wedding. As time rolled along, Wallick added William Farnum and two more horses, "Texas", and "Arabian Jim", to his company. Farnum was later to demonstrate his artistry as a "he-man" type of lover in the movies. Perhaps it would not be too far shy of the mark to credit Wallick and his herd of trained horses as the originators of the movie and TV westerns which are the daily diet of so many film-watchers of this day and time.[2]

There is likewise a remote possibility that O. Henry could have picked up an idea or so from Wallick about horses as props of the Western scene. Cows are so few in the author's outdoor stories that it would hardly have been a surprise to discover that the number of horses had been kept at a minimum. We know the cows are there, of course; we see the pokes as they loll in camp and meet the kings and barons as they take their ease, but the bovine quadrupeds themselves are off-stage somewhere, perhaps grazing on the contiguous meadows or nooning in the shade by the water-holes. This is why the reader finds such a delightful novelty in old McAllister's daughter Santa's exploit in the corral; here we see the little headstrong queen of the kine actually slip in among the Sussex herd and adroitly ensnare and brand the milk-white cow. Here in "Hearts and Crosses" is the only herd of cattle we are allowed to go among in the whole range of O. Henry's Texas stories; but as we travel from story to story we meet horses galore.

To begin with, there is Sam Galloway's pony with the Dante Alighieri face, and the mile-an-hour steed of old man Ellison ("The Last of the Troubadours"); there is the sympathetic bronc of Judson Odom in "The Pimienta Pancakes"; Jud's bronc, a cow-pony by training, shares his master's dislike for snoozers; there are the horses that Solomon Mills buys saddles for in "Seats

2 William F. Cody (Buffalo Bill) cannot be overlooked in the history of Western melodrama. He and Texas Jack Omohundro were seen in San Antonio in their melodrama, *Life on the Border*, as early as November 27, 1875. San Antonio *Express* (November 28, 1875).

of the Haughty". Maybe we should not count Mills' ponies since they are off-stage somewhere, perhaps with the cows. And we must mention the pair of Spanish ponies of Ross Hargis's buckboard and the mounts of the galloping centaurs of "Hygeia at the Solito"; and the buckboard greys that bring Ranse Truesdell and Curly to the Rancho Cibolo ("The Higher Abdication"); the speckled roan and the loping dun that carry the Cisco Kid and Lieut. Sandridge to their destinies in "The Caballero's Way"; the four stout horses of Bildad Rose in "The Sphinx Apple"; Donder and Blitzen (which, to paraphrase a phrase of Macbeth's, can go for horses in the catalogue) and the unnamed mounts of Hondo Bill and his gang in "A Chaparral Prince"; and there is certainly Hot Tamales, prancing and solicitiously mindful, who saves Ronny Briscoe from embarrassment in "Art and the Bronco"; and let us not forget (although we must mention silently) the long-legged, curved necked roan that takes the Llano Kid out of danger in "A Double-Dyed Deceiver".

More important rôles in other compositions are assigned to other equine actors. In this regard we mention the wild, creamcolored Spanish ponies and their feather-weight buckboard that hurry Ted Westlake and Octavia Beaupree breathlessly over the grassy prairies to love and happiness ("Madame Bo-Peep, of the Ranches"); the two Kentucky bays that perform a similar office for Jeff and Mame in "Cupid à la Carte"; Vaminos and Dancer, the pair of ponies that bring Yenna Curtis and Ranse Truesdell to their trysting place under the oaks ("The Higher Abdication"); the paint and fleabitten sorrel of the two wooers, Madison Lane and Johnny Mc Roy (the latter the Frio Kid), hero and villain in "A Chaparral Christmas Gift"; Fly and Bess, ponies who stand fire so nicely for Littlefield and Nancy Derwent in the pastoral idyl, "One Dollar's Worth"; the two mounts that provide a setting for the love-affair of Josefa O'Donnell and Ripley Givens in "The Princess and the Puma"; and one must not omit Belshazzar, another fleabitten sorrel, who brings the repentant Webb Yeager back to his Queen in "Hearts and Crosses"; nor the four horses it takes to consummate the act of revenge in the feud-story, "A Technical Error": the two Kentucky-bred mounts of Sam Durkee, rightful avenger, with his recording supernumerary, and the mustangs that pull the yellow-wheeled buggy of Ben Tatum and Ella Baynes, murderer and the girl he had stolen, partners in illicit love.

VI

THE FRIENDSHIP STORIES

O. Henry could have found more interest in Bartley Campbell's *My Partner* than in any of Wallick's fantastic melodramas. *My Partner* was staged for the first time in San Antonio at Turner Hall on November 10, 1882. The Campbell play, like Bret Harte's *Tennessee's Partner*, is an account of the friendship of two miners. In the Campbell drama, the two miners are Joe Saunders and his partner, Ned Singleton, the false lover.[1] Saunders, the hero of the drama, is as much a man of honor as he is a friend; he feels himself compelled to force his partner to vow that he will marry Mary Brandon, the woman Singleton has wronged, and also the woman whom Saunders loves. In persuading Joe to make his vow, Saunders uses his pistol. This act of persuasion is of note as the only instance in the drama where a character, for any reason whatsoever, resorts to the employment of firearms. Campbell's limitation in the use of side-arms could be called a bit of "toning down" of violence in border drama. There is a murder in the play, but it is accomplished without the firing of a shot: villain Scraggs kills Ned Singleton with Saunder's knife. Ned, despite his guilt as a seducer, does not hesitate to defend the honor of both Mary Brandon and Joe Saunders. His attempt to do this costs him his life.

Saunders is brought to trial for the murder of his former partner. Meanwhile, when Mary's father hears of her frivolous pre-marital act, he raises all manner of Cain, cursing and venting

---

[1] Arthur Hobson Quinn says that, "There is no question that *My Partner* is true to the life it portrayed . . .". *A History of American Drama, from the Civil War to the Present Day*, V, 122.

his spleen most horribly. Saunders, to soften the misery of the poor girl, says that he will marry her. With the rope virtually round his neck, he and Mary are made man and wife. He weds her, one might say, to save her honor, out of respect for his departed friend, and to satisfy his own amorous impulses. No man, certainly has shown greater love than this. There may be, of course, some who might look at the action in a different light.

Towards the end of Act IV, the heathen Chinee of the piece discovers the villain Scragg's bloody shirt in the well where the scoundrel had thrown the garment. Scragg's villainy is established with this piece of evidence. The noose round Joe Saunders' neck now becomes a rope of sand and dissolves clean away. As the curtain falls, this honorable hero is able to tell Mary that "our love will illuminate our lives forever".

A phase of the plot of *My Partner* is suggestive of a situation in Kotzebue's *The Stranger*, a drama which may be thought of as one of the "bigamy" pieces popular on the stage in Europe and America in the nineteenth century.[2] In *The Stranger*, as in the Campbell melodrama, it is a friend of the wronged man who seduces his lady-love. In the Kotzebue drama, Count Charles Walbourg (or the Stranger, as he is presented to the audience) has his pretty sixteen-year-old wife led astray by a false friend. Three years later the estranged pair meet again – the husband now an unsettled misanthrope, and the wife, posing as a Mrs. Haller, a melancholy and lonesome penitent; at this encounter their children, a young boy and girl, are brought before them. Both parents soften in the presence of the young ones and "rush into an embrace". Just prior to this touching show of affection, it appears that the couple, mindful now of the great barrier between themselves, would forego further happiness on earth, and be content "to meet again in a better world". Some producers of the play on the American stage considered the reconciliation scene as detracting from the strength of the piece and omitted it. Mrs.

[2] August Frederic von Kotzebue (1791-1819) was a German dramatist. His *Menschenhass und Reue* was for a long time popular on the English-speaking stage as *The Stranger*. Maturin's *Bertram*, and Mrs. Henry Wood's *East Lynne*, other bigamy dramas, will not be considered here since in both plays the seducer is not a friend of the protagonist.

Haller's transgression has taken place long before the action of the drama begins, and the lady is revealed as a charming, high-minded woman, who readily wins one's admiration. On the other hand Campbell's Mary Brandon appears as a palpably weak creature, incapable of making the proper distinctions; we find Mary begging her seducer to marry her to protect her honor. It is Joe Saunders who performs this office for her; and it must be said that Joe's concept of this virtue seems damnably unconventional. It is this peculiar notion of a hero's make-up that O. Henry playfully satirizes in his friendship stories.[3]

"The Handbook of Hymen" can best be understood in the light of what we know about Campbell's *My Partner* and Harte's *Tennessee's Partner*. Although written professedly to show that the educational system of the U. S. should be in the hands of the weather bureau, the story, like *The Stranger*, is a variation on the theme of friendship. Idaho Green and Sanderson Pratt are miners and inseparable friends. While prospecting for gold in the Bitter Root mountains they are snowbound for a month in a cabin.

"If you want to instigate the art of manslaughter", says Sanderson Pratt, narrator of the story, "just shut two men up in an eighteen by twenty-foot cabin for a month."

Before their spell of confinement is over, the two are cooking their grub on opposite sides of the fireplace and have stopped speaking to one another. Finally, Idaho, while poking round with a stick on a shelf which he finds out of his reach knocks down two books. One proves to be a copy of Fitzgerald's "Rubaiyat", and the other an information handbook called "Herkimer's Handbook of Useful Information". The partners play a game of seven-up to determine who will make the first selection of the items found. Idaho Green wins and takes the "Rubaiyat". His choice leaves the "Herkimer" for Sanderson Pratt. The men calm down now to enjoy the luxury of their respective "finds". Their riled-up tempers are so mollified by their studies that they are again on speaking terms by the time they leave the cabin.

---

[3] Tolstoy lets his pretty and virtuous Natasha Rostof, while engaged to Prince Andrey Bolskonsy, become infatuated with the rake, Anatole Kuragin. (Leo Tolstoy, *War and Peace*, trans. Constance Garnett, Part Eight.)

After the snow thaws, the two leave the quarters where they have been so long confined and soon thereafter make $8000 a piece in a strike across the Montana line. Not long after this piece of luck they go down to the little village of Rosa to enjoy their newly acquired wealth; in Rosa they soon join twenty-two other suitors who have laid seige to the heart of the queen of Rosa society, a widow, Mrs. D. Ormond Sampson. Sandy Pratt plies the good lady with statistics gleaned from his "Herkimer"; Idaho Green quotes random passages from his "Rubaiyat". The scholarly method of courting of these friendly rivals furnishes the humor of the story. The widow seems deeply impressed from the beginning with Pratt's statistics. Green's poetical quotes, on the other hand, apparently misfire all along. He insults the lady one day when he recites a well-known passage.

> A Book of Verses underneath the Bough,
> A Jug of Wine, a Loaf of Bread – and Thou
> Beside me singing in the Wilderness –
> Oh, Wilderness were Paradise enow!

The quotation shocks the widow and she runs to Pratt with a tale of what she considers his friend's indecency. Pratt, although somewhat blind to the meaning of the verses himself, is too faithful a partner to say anything uncomplimentary of his friend; he chooses rather to come back strong with his statistics.

"Though it is warm here, we should remember that at the equator the line of perpetual frost is at an altitude of fifteen thousand feet", he tells her. At the sound of her lover's voice Mrs. Sampson instantly forgets her grievance.

"Oh, Mr. Pratt", the lady says, "it's such a comfort to hear you say them beautiful facts...!"

The cleverest stroke of the author's satire occurs when he represents Pratt as winning the heart of the widow by carrying her out of her burning mansion-home and reviving her by putting flaxseed in her eye. In his haste to consult Herkimer, Pratt turns over two pages in the book and reads the wrong antidote (as a physician who arrives on the scene shows him), but the remedy pleases the patient, and brings about the desired results.

We have in the "Handbook of Hymen", as in "My Partner", two devoted friends who court the same woman, but O. Henry uses the "Herkimer" as a factor in the protagonist's winning his goal. This book, a small compendium of useful facts, is similar to many that were actually in print during the latter half of the nineteenth century. One such book, currently extant, is "Conklin's Handy Manual of Useful Information and Atlas of the World". The subtitle shows the work to be "A Universal Hand-Book for Ready Reference". The book was compiled by Professor George W. Conklin of Hamilton University and Copyright in 1887 by George W. Ogilvie.

In Conklin is the statement: "The deepest coal mine in the world is at Killingworth, England, near Newcastle..."; and on another page: "The nearest fixed star is 16,000,000 miles distant, and takes three years for its light to reach the earth."

Sanderson Pratt tells Mrs. Sampson that "the deepest mine in the world is at Killingworth, near Newcastle"; and that the big star she sees is "sixty-six billions of miles distant. It took thirty-six years for its light to reach us." Both Herkimer and Conklin tell what to do before the doctor comes, name the longest tunnel in the world, and give the heights of the principal mountains on all continents. In Conklin, however, there is no mention of the number of hairs on a blond lady's head, as in Herkimer; nor does Conklin give any figures on the length of a person's perspiratory ducts when placed end to end. Conklin may perhaps have considered such anatomical facts as lacking in appeal to the general reader.

"Telemachus, Friend", shows a closer resemblance to the Campbell melodrama than does the story we have just considered. Telemachus Hicks, protagonist of this narrative of friendship, who seems to be a part of all he has known, and Paisley Fish, blunt, uncouth, and not especially knowing in the ways of men, have for seven years "mined, ranched, and sold patent churns", presumably as partners. Although the two are friends to an amount one can hardly imagine and have "had days of Damon and nights of Pythias", their amicable relationship nearly falls asunder when they come down to the town of Los Piños and soon afterward declare their intentions of winning the heart and hand of a café proprietress, the widow Jessup. Unlike Gisippus (of the Titus-Gisippus combination), who believes that the laws of love annul even the divine laws, the two partners, on the suggestion of Telemachus Hicks, agree to put the bonds of their attachment to an open test: Hicks proposes to Fish that the two do their courting in each other's presence. Such a manner of courtship is not without precedent. We learn from Desdemona that Othello sometimes brought Cassio along when he came to woo her; but of course Cassio was merely an attendant and not a rival of his general.[4] Hicks' wooing-scheme can be considered as a playful take-off on the brotherly comradeship of the Bartley Campbell-Joe Saunders-Ned Singleton variety, as well as on Othello's courtship of Senator Brabantio's daughter. Othello "in the show" wins the "duke's daughter", but Fish, using similar tactics, fails to impress the widow Jessup. A reader, too, would be more inclined to admit that Fish's "skinning match of dead cows with Pieface Lumley in '95" seems a mite nearer the truth than Othello's tale about the men with their heads beneath their shoulders. Hicks declares that his rival uses a mixture of the talk turned out by Rider Haggard, Lew Dockstader, and Dr. Parkhurst. From the samples of Fish's speech that are offered us we can observe that his sweet nothings of love do sound remarkably like Dockstader's blackface minstrel chatter; although it can be said as well of Hicks, that his formula for picking up a woman's hand and holding it so as not "to let her know that you think she knows you have the least idea she is aware you are holding her hand" sounds a wee bit like blackface "bones" Lew Dockstader himself, revealing his "darktown" love philosophy to the interlocutor.

It is clear from the first that the widow Jessup gives the nod to the amorous Hicks. And since this is apparent, some might wonder why she is tolerant of Fish's absurdities for so long a time. Right in the midst of the love avowals of the two suitors, the lady speaks out in sobering words that explain her position.

"Mr. Hicks, . . . if it wasn't but for one thing, I'd ask you to

4 Desdemona says that Michael Cassio "came a-wooing" with Othello "many a time". *Othello*, III, iii, 80-81.

hike yourself down the gulch and never disresume your visits to my house."

And when Hicks asks what the one thing is, she has this answer, "You're too good a friend not to make a good husband."

The seriousness of the remark almost takes the sting out of the satire. Mrs. Jessup definitely sees the light much sooner than Bartley Campbell's Mary Brandon.

The synonymous gallivantery of the two unconventional Romeos seems fully as decorous in a gaily critical kind of story as Joe Saunder's excuse for Mary's transgression does in a melodrama of grave tone.

It is left to Hicks to show to what an utterly ridiculous extreme friendship between man and man can be carried. A month after the two partners have made their compact, Hicks marries Mrs. Jessup with due pomp and ceremony in the Los Piños Methodist Church. The bridegroom balks as the rituals are about to begin. He feels honor-bound to wait for his pal, Paisley Fish. This creature comes galloping up after awhile, buttoning a cuff and explaining that he had had a heap of trouble finding a boiled shirt to suit his tastes. The bride-soon-to-be shows her disgust at this untoward circumstance by snapping at her lover with her eyes.

Some hours later on (at ten o'clock at night, that is) Hicks is sitting with his boots off in the front door of his little cottage enjoying the cool air. Bye and bye the lights go off in the front room, and Mrs. Hicks is heard to call out, "Ain't you coming in soon, Lem?"

Hicks rouses out of his reverie at her words and replies, "Durn me if I wasn't waiting for old Paisley to . . ."

Mrs. Hicks stops his utterance with a mutilating blow on the left ear, at the same time terminating the compact between the two partners. Regardless of whatever else we deduce from this violent conjugal blow, we can surely say that the woman in this triangle knows her way about better than Mary Brandon. Perhaps Sut Lovingood's words aptly fit the situation: "Widders am a special means, . . ., for ripenin green men, killin off weak ones, and makin' 'ternally happy the sound ones'." [5]

---

[5]   G. W. Harris, "Mrs. Yardley's Quilting", *Sut Lovingood*, p. 134.

The little touch of the slapstick that ends the sequence of events in the story is a conventional twist in comical extravaganzas. Charles Hale Hoyt sprinkled such devices throughout his satirical farce-comedies. In proof of how widely in vogue was the practice, we mention the barrel of beer that explodes and splatters "suds" over the raiders in *A Temperance Town*: Will Peak has his coat torn and his face disfigured; Kneeland Pray, a scheming druggist, has his face blackened; Dr. Sawyer loses one side of his whiskers.[6] And does not George Washington Harris resort to similar farcical devices to enliven his Sut Lovingood sketches? Sicily Burns blows Sut up with soda to cure his puppy love;[7] and old man Yardley plants the "vamp" and "sole" of one of his brogans on Sut's fundament – "a back action earth quake", the victim calls it – to kick Sut out of the Yardley home.[8]

We are reluctant to dismiss "Telemachus, Friend" without a comment on what the author makes Telemachus Hicks say about the "moral surface of nature". The partner, while sitting beside the widow Jessup on the first evening of his joint courtship with Paisley Fish gives a thumbnail sketch of nature as he had found it.

That evening was certainly a case in point. The moon was attending to business in the section of the sky where it belonged, and there was a kind of conspicuous hullabaloo going on in the bushes between the bullbats and orioles and jack-rabbits and other feathered insects of the forest. And the wind out of the mountains was singing like a jew's-harp in the pile of old tomato-cans by the railroad track.

This bit of playful raillery is more in the Sut Lovingood vein than in the manner of Bret Harte. There's no suggestion of the neo-pathetic fallacy in these words.[9] Nature, as Hicks observes its manifestations, has no consciousness of man, much less any sympathy for him; nor are the sounds of nature especially pleasing. It could be that the motions of Hicks' spirit have an Erebus-like

---

6 Charles H. Hoyt, "A Temperance Town", Act II.
7 G. W. Harris, "Blown Up with Soda", *op. cit.*, p. 75.
8 G. W. Harris, "Mrs. Yardley's Quilting", *op. cit.*, 148.
9 The neo-pathetic fallacy is much less acceptable as a literary device than the ordinary pathetic fallacy, as defined by Ruskin. The former strains the reader's credulity almost to the breaking point.

dullness; and it could be, too, that O. Henry was gently ridiculing such an instance of the neo-pathetic fallacy as is found in these lines from "The Luck of Roaring Camp".

Nature was his nurse and playfellow. For him she would let slip between the leaves golden shafts of sunlight that fell just within his grasp; she would send wandering breezes to visit him with the balm of bay and resinous gum; to him the tall redwoods nodded familiarly and sleepily, the bumblebees buzzed, and the rooks cawed a slumbrous accompaniment.

"The Friendly Call" could conceivably entitle O. Henry to the designation of a Y. M. C. A. Boccaccio. In this story Simon Bell defines a friend as "one you can deal with on a strict reciprocity basis", as he and George Ringo have always done. But the two men seem to be friends only so far as "feminine attachments" go. In other aspects of an amicable relationship, their attitude toward each other, unlike that of Gisippus toward Titus, is unquestionably peculiar.[10] The two Boccaccio characters certainly have more "personal use" for each other's ways than do Ringo and Bell; the latter pair demonstrate the true values of their attachment by relieving each other from time to time of the wifely presence of the former Mrs. De Clinton. We cannot conceive of Simon Bell defending his position with the philosophical astuteness that Titus Quintius Fulvus shows when he appears before the family and friends of Sophronia; Bell takes the "woman in the case" off the hands of Ringo in a somewhat perfunctory manner. He appears to feel that it is his duty as a friend to execute the trust and he stands by ready to perform the function. Herein of course lies the humor of the piece. The author toys flippantly with aspects of a delicate business that Boccaccio and Bartley Campbell treat with seriousness.

It is interesting to note, likewise, that Bell tests Ringo's loyalty with a "calf carcass" battered and done up to resemble a mutilated corpse; the despondent Gisippus claims credit for a murder he did not commit; and Titus disputes this claim out of loyalty to his sacrificing friend; the falsely accused Joe Saunders, near death

[10] Giovanni Boccaccio, Eighth Story, Tenth Day, *The Decameron*.

because of the murder of his friend, Ned Singleton, is saved from the gallows by a streak of luck at the last minute.

Of the four stories O. Henry developed on the miner-partner motif, "The Ransom of Mack" shows the greatest diversity of elements. Mack Lonsbury and Andy, the author narrator, seem to be more like business partners than friends of the Damon and Pythias order. After a career as miners, the two friends settle down in the little town of Piña with a competence of $40,000 each, to enjoy for a while the simple life they both have long yearned for. Mack is happy as he pours over the pages of Buckle's *History of Civilization* and Andy appears equally satisfied with his Sep Winner's *Self-Instructor for the Banjo*. The "heathen Chinee" is with the men in their retirement but is reduced to a mere functionary who is hardly more than a name; actually, the Chinaman may be called a "factor" who contributes to the happy existence of Lonsbury as this person goes about the business of satisfying himself in his simple way; he is a sort of counterbalance to Andy's cuckoo clock, which is a contributory accessory to the latter's circumscribed notion of happiness.

A notable variation on the friendship theme is the way the woman is brought into the story. Mack one day asks Andy if he is "much apprised in the habits and policies of women folks". Following this query, the two men indulge in a quantity of hyperbolic verbiage on the subject of woman, from which discussion the reader can deduce some very positive conclusions. Mack confesses a complete ignorance of the sex and makes it "fairly" clear that he is too old to develop any interest whatsoever in women. Andy, on the other hand, declares positively that only a man who understands women can take care of himself in this world; and he ends his statement by declaring himself to be such a man.

Andy one day is called away from Piña to attend to mining business in New Mexico. On his return, he finds Mack, who says that he has been elected justice of the peace, dressed in patent-leather shoes, a white silk vest and a high silk hat. From his partner's fancy dress, and a certain rather manifest coyishness of manner, Andy falsely concludes that his sharer of the *vita simplex* is afflicted with what he calls the "Mary-Jane infirmity".

Andy is reprimanding the new justice of the peace for his folly, when a young woman passes by the two as they stand talking on the sidewalk. Mack snickers and blushes as he declares, "I'm going to marry the young lady who just passed to-night." Andy is now satisfied that his partner is about to end his days of bachelorhood. It is this meddler's exaggerated confidence in himself as an authority on womankind that prompts him to jump to the conclusion that Mack is about to become the husband of Miss Rebosa Redd. As it turns out, of course, Lonsbury, as justice of the peace is merely going to perform the ceremony. The revelation of the egocentric's error constitutes the "snap" or denouement of the story.[11] An ingenious element of this story is the appearance of "the woman" in the piece as a mere hypotenuse instead of a definite clear-cut angle of the eternal triangle, a variant that contributes pleasantly to a time-worn theme.

[11]   The ending of this story reminds the reader of how Rufe Tatum pulls the wool over the eyes of the credulous Jeff Peters in "The Ethics of Pig". Similarly, the over-confident Judson Odom loses out in his love venture in "The Pimienta Pancakes".

VII

COWMEN, REAL AND IMAGINARY

There has seldom been a more pronounced or more genuine comradeship in a segment of American society than that which formed a bond of union among Texas cattlemen in the post-Civil War period. Most of these men had fought a losing fight in the Confederate service, often as soldiers in the same commands, and as a result of their battle-field associations found solace as well as help in making common cause in the new enterprise that fate had placed before them. Among these soldiers of the Confederate cause, all of whom became prominent in the cattle industry, may be mentioned Major Seth Mabry; Captain E. B. Millet and his twin brother Alonzo Millet; Northern-born John and Thomas Dewees, who served under Captain E. B. Millet; Colonel D. H. Snider of Round Rock; Colonel Dillard R. Fant; "Cattle King" James D. Reed, who lost an arm in battle; W. A. "Buck" Pettus, who had also been with Ben Milam in the capture of San Antonio; Captain Charles Schreiner, born in Alsace-Lorraine, who was four years with the C. S. A.; Major George W. Littlefield, a lieutenant in Terry's Texas Rangers at eighteen years of age; and Columbus C. "Lum" Slaughter, who came to own one million acres of land to qualify as the "biggest" tax-payer in Texas.

A fine illustration of a cowman's friendship and loyalty is furnished in the account of how Bill Butler, ex-Confederate and Karnes County rancher, at great risk to his own comfort and safety, helped two friends, Tom O'Connor and Buck Pettus, recover cattle from a gang of thieves. On the occasion referred to, Butler was on his way back home with his own cattle which he had forced the robbers to release. Learning from his friends that

they were on a mission similar to the one he had just come back
from, Butler joined them in retrieving their stolen stock. Mr.
Butler's close association with Major Seth Mabry in sending close
to 100,000 head of cattle up the trail is further proof of how well
two comrades could work together for the profit of both.[1]

O. Henry's Major Tom Kingman had learned of the goodness
of man back in the days when the high price of cattle had established him as a man of means in his community. He had been
mule-driver, had fought Indians, had served under General Forrest
at Fort Pillow and at Shiloh, was later a trail-driver, and after-
wards a cattleman. At the time the story, "Friends in San
Rosario", begins, we find Kingman president of the First National
Bank of San Rosario. Bank examiner Nettlewick visits the little
town to inspect Kingman's bank, as well as a rival bank headed
by the Major's old crony, Bob Buckley. Nettlewick wishes to
hurry his job at both houses of finance so that he will not be long
detained in the little uninteresting Texas town. The examiner's
visit has come at a time when Buckley is short $18,000 which he
has let out on a loan. Through a messenger, Kingman learns of his
friend's plight and resorts to a ruse to hold Nettlewick until funds
to relieve the embarrassed Buckley come in on the 10:30 narrow-
gage. Kingman detains the perplexed Nettlewick with a fantastic
story of the misadventure of a sleep-walker. The bank president
keeps the examiner engaged with his yarn until he learns by a
prearranged sign – a drawn window shade – that the train has
come in on time to bring the sum of money to relieve Buckley.

Such is the story O. Henry tells of how a banker, an ex-cow-
poke, comes to the aid of a friend who has been a mite indiscreet
in the matter of making a loan.

It was nothing unusual, of course, for a cattleman to found a
bank. George F. Hindes of Frio county, just north of La Salle,
organized the Pearsall National Bank in 1903. Mr. Hindes' life,
as he tells us, indicates that he had as much spunk and guts as
the fictional creations he could have inspired.[2] Alabama-born
Thomas Jefferson Moore, one of whose ranches was in Webb

[1]   *Trail Drivers of Texas*, II, 716-717.
[2]   *Ibid.*, 821.

county just south of La Salle, made several trips up the trail, became prosperous, and, among other interests, established a bank in the town of Llano. There were so many other cowmen of affluence who went into the banking business that one might be inclined to call such a course a settled custom with these gentlemen. We take passing note of George H. Reynolds, founder of a bank at Albany, Texas; Major George W. Littlefield, of the American National Bank of Austin; and R. R. Russell, with interests in banks in Ballinger and San Antonio.[3]

Long Bill Longley (in "A Call Loan"), graduate of camp and trail, is O. Henry's best-rounded portrait of a successful cattleman. Long Bill's Bar Circle brand is much like the apple brand of cattleman R. G. (Dick) Head, a mark that many people mistook for a bar circle. Like Longley, Dick Head rose to a proud eminence in the cow trade by "luck and thrift", as well as, of course, by other qualities.[4] That Longley, the creature of an author's fancy, is likewise credited with a cool head and a quick eye for strays in no way detracts from the naturalness of the portrait.

Longley, who has organized the First National Bank of Chaparosa, is distracted by an untimely visit of bank examiner J. Edgar Todd. Todd soon discovers that banker Longley has made an irregular "call loan" to patron Tom Merwin. Longley naively explains to the examiner that Merwin had a chance to make $7 a round on two thousand head of two-year-old steers, but lacked $10,000 to finish out the $16,000 he needed to swing the deal. Unlike examiner Nettlewick, Todd offers Longley a loop-hole. He lets the bank president have until noon the following day to gather up the necessary funds.

Tom Merwin, displaying a willingness to illustrate the oft-repeated axiom that an outlaw is merely a good cowboy gone bad, arms himself with a brace of single-action sixes, masks his face in a black handkerchief, and makes ready to rob the narrow-gage train as its engine takes water at a tank. Merwin has learned from Cooper of a private bank of the town that that firm is shipping $15,000 out "that night" on the railroad. For that reason

---

3 *Ibid.*, 360, 671, 700, 800.
4 *Ibid.*, 734.

Cooper cannot advance any money to Merwin; and the latter is willing to resort to any measure to save a friend so dear to him that "he can call the blood out of my veins". Longley, however, follows Merwin to his water-tank hiding-place and keeps his friend from carrying out the rash act he has planned. Everything turns out well when it develops that Merwin's brother Ed has come back home on the train which Tom would have robbed; Ed brings with him $29,000, a sum a few figures in excess of the amount Tom needs to square himself with the First National Bank.

It was common practice among cowmen bankers to lend money to trusted patrons without security. This chronicler recalls a time when a respected stockman friend of his out Pecos way borrowed $30,000 from bankers D. Sullivan and Company, of San Antonio, with only his word as collateral. "Danny" Sullivan got his money back in the allotted time. Of course Sullivan's was a private bank and not subject to the same regulations that govern national banking institutions.

This same Daniel Sullivan could, however, put a Nettlewick-Todd squeeze on a customer when he thought such an urgency would serve his ends. Chris Emmett tells an engaging little yarn about how Sullivan demanded from Shanghai Pierce payment in gold on $50,000 in notes that were coming due.[5] With a better directed zeal than O. Henry's Tom Merwin, old Shang travelled about through various towns calling out for gold. He collected the needed sum and delivered it in due time, an act that enabled the wily old cowman to turn the tables on his erstwhile ranch partner.

From such practices as those set down on the pages of fiction or recorded in the annals of Southwestern finance we can deduce that banking in the eighties and nineties was "cussedly" informal, to say the least.

Many of O. Henry's cowmen have lives not altogether different from those of the men who trailed the longhorn to market and

---

[5] *Shanghai Pierce, A True Likeness*, XIX.

fenced in the grassy domain of the Southwest with the new-fangled "vicious" and "obvious" barbed wire of Messrs. Glidden, Haisch, and Ellwood.[6] It is not merely a coincidence that the author represents "Kiowa" Truesdell in "The Higher Abdication" as having come to Texas in 1855 from the lowlands of Mississippi; nor can we believe that Curtis Raidler in "Hygeia at the Solito" is an Alabamian by birth simply because his progenitor was at a loss to find another name for the rancher's natal state.[7] O. Henry could well have given these personages their birthplaces by design.

One of the best known and wealthiest cattlemen in the country Sydney Porter came to know so well was William J. Slaughter. Slaughter was born in the state of Mississippi in 1835 and died near Friotown, Frio County, August 31, 1906. In 1855 he had established his home in the unorganized County of La Salle. Here he brought his family to live. Slaughter returned to his ranch a poor man from four years of service in the Confederate army. "For eight years for them [Slaughter and his family] it was worse than war. During the entire time the worst type of outlaws and hostile Indians murdered and plundered to such an extent as to render life and property insecure."[8] Through unceasing effort Mr. Slaughter in time gained great wealth. The landed domain known originally as the Slaughter Ranch was one of the largest in Western Texas.

In "The Higher Abdication", elderly "Kiowa" Truesdell, in virtual retirement when the reader meets him, spends a good part of his time reading in a great wicker chair under a big oil lamp. He has fewer children than Mr. Cattleman Slaughter is said to have had; in fact, as it turns out, he has but one; and since that child, when the story opens, has long before departed from the

---

[6] For a comprehensive treatment of the subject of barbed wire see Henry D. and Frances T. McCallum, *The Wire That Fenced the West*.

[7] The truculent King James is considerably mollified when he discovers that old man Ellison is related to the Jackson country Reeves of Mississippi. "The Last of the Troubadours", *Works*, II, 818. Calliope Catesby, while not exactly a cowman, and not exactly an admirable figure, shows that he has a spark of good in his makeup when his mother comes out to visit him from Alabama. "The Reformation of Calliope", *Works*, I, 265, 266.

[8] *The Trail Drivers of Texas*, II, 608.

parental nest, the venerable cowman wants to make his adoptive son Ranse heir to all of his estate, real and personal. For a long time Ranse has thought that he was Truesdell's rightful heir; but by accident he finds an old letter that tells him the truth about himself: he is an adopted son. It is with interest that we note that the antecedents of "Old Kiowa" are remarkably similar to those of Mr. William J. Slaughter.

"Old Kiowa" tells Ranse:

> Son, I've lived for you. I've fought wolves and Indians and worse white men to protect you. . . . Later on I've worked to pile up dollars that will be yours. You'll be a rich man, Ranse, when my chunk goes out. I've made you.[9]

This is plain talk, untinged with romance. We can easily imagine that Truesdell talks much like any one of the many Mississippi-born Texas land-owners might have talked to a son. And of course there were many with such an origin. A cursory examination of the sketches in The Trial Drivers of Texas shows that Texas ranchers from Mississippi far outnumbered those of any other state. Two of the most notable Mississippians who gained prominence in the cattle industry in Texas were Major George W. Littlefield and Colonel James F. Ellison.[10] Littlefield became a banker and contributed largely to the state university; and Ellison, with his partner Dewees, sent as many cattle up the trail to the North as any other man in the business.

When Curtis Raidler, native of Alabama, in "Hygeia at the Solito", picks up the consumptive "Cricket" McGuire, and out of compassion carries this ex-featherweight pug, ex-jockey, and tout down to his La Salle ranch he is doing a benevolent act that was the common practice of Southwest Texas ranchers in real life. If Porter had sought an inspiration for the creation of Raidler, he could have found it in the person of Mont Woodward, a cowman who dispensed hospitality at the headquarters of his extensive land holdings west of Frio Town in a county north of La Salle.[11] In

---

[9]   "The Higher Abdication", Works, I, 182.
[10]   For a sketch of Major Littlefield see Trail Drivers of Texas, II, 700; for Colonel J. F. Ellison see ibid., I, 476.
[11]   Trail Drivers of Texas, II, 680.

fact, as his biographer tells us, it was the generous disposition of the man that led to his death. He was brutally murdered and robbed by two tramps whom he had entertained at supper.

As for Alabama-born cowmen, with large landed estates near the Dull, Hall, and Dull holdings (where young Sydney Porter made his home for a few years), we may mention Thomas Jefferson Moore, with acreage in Webb country, south of La Salle, and George F. Hindes, whose 40,000 acre spread was east of La Salle on San Miguel creek.[12] The San Miguel is a stream of water that engaged the attention of Porter. He makes use of it in at least two stories: "I was punching for old Bill Toomey, on the San Miguel", says Judson Odom in "The Pimienta Pancakes"; "Up to last month we owned four sections... down on the San Miguel", explains Solly Mills in "Seats of the Haughty".

Another well known cowman, a rancher of La Salle County, was William C. Irvin. Irvin's father was from Alabama. The Irvin ranch was made up of 60,000 acres of land east of Cotulla, extending to the very edge of the town. William C. Irvin had made seven trips up the Chisholm trail by 1875.[13]

Curtis Raidler, like all other of his creator's cattle folk, is a tall, well-built blond, with grey or blue eyes, a man of obvious Anglo-Saxon origin. McGuire, who is somewhat on the abbreviated pattern, calls Raidler "telegraph pole". The cowman's tastes are simple but wholesome, and like the counterparts after whom he is fashioned, he has a knack of making money from cows and, as a consequence, is "well-fixed". He knows horses as well as he does cows, is addicted to the vice of smoking, and for a sport, besides horsemanship, seems to follow the chase. The east room of Raidler's Nueces County home (which the author indicates is typical of the cow country) reflects the owner's manner of life. Raidler does not appear to be a jot interested in the Fitzsimmons-Peter Maher pugilistic contest, a fracas that had separated McGuire from his last few dollars; like Mont Woodward, whom we have previously cited, the young rancher is activated simply by

12 *Ibid.*, 712, 821.
13 *Ibid.*, 619-621.

the generous impulses of his nature.[14] This is the main theme of the story. Another motivating impulse is the theory, quite commonly accepted in southwest Texas at the time, that a tubercular victim could regain his health only from mother nature. The restoration could be accomplished by staying out of doors and passing as much time as possible literally down on the earth. "Hygeia at the Solito" shows how a generous man restores primal vigor to a consumptive by the application of the simplest of all remedies.

As the action of "The Higher Abdication" progresses, it develops that Ranse Truesdell is in love with Yenna Curtis, daughter of one of the Mississippi Curtises, with whom the Truesdells have been feuding since long before the two families came out to the wilds of Texas. And here it might be well to digress for a while to make a few comments on feuding both as a literary motif and as a way of life. We cannot let ourselves quarrel with the idea that Mississippi is not just as suitable a setting for a feud as the dark and bloody ground of Kentucky. Certainly no thoughts of that sort appear to bother Ranse. Like Romeo, he knows that love will find a way, and it does just that for him and Yenna. He wins her simply by proving to "Kiowa" that he is not a Truesdell. Circumstances make the solution easy for him. Bloodshed is avoided as a result and we do not have the nasty tragedy that ruins the earthly careers of Romeo and Juliet – as well as the lives of many of the Graingerfords (in "Huckleberry Finn"), when daughter Sophia runs away with Harney Shepherdson. The Capulet-Montague quarrel costs innocent Mercutio and meddling Tybalt their lives as well as proving to be a disgrace to the whole city of Verona. The Graingerford-Shepherdson affair, however, has a broader and more devastating effect than that: that is, if we are to believe certain fantastic critics of Twain's masterpiece. These interpreters declare that the feud in question is an indict-

---

[14] In 1896, Bob Fitzsimmons knocked out Peter Maher, champion of Ireland, in one minute flat, including handshakes. The fight occurred opposite Langtry, Texas, on a sand bar in the Rio Grande. Roy Bean had promoted the fight and Governor Culberson had tried to stop it. Frank X. Tolbert, *An Informal History of Texas*, p. 23.

ment of the way of life of the entire South. Other scholars, more modest in their appraisals, assert that the Twain feud is a transposed Kentucky outrage that has no business at all happening in Arkansas.

A glance here and there into the histories of actual American feuds is both revealing and profitable to the curious reader. As we delve into the chronicled facts we find ourselves wondering how far away from reality the inventors of these contending opposites of fiction have strayed. Let us focus our attention on some of the best known feuds. The real McCoy-Hatfield conflict was a kind of war of the roses, except that it was a hog figuring in the more recent disturbance instead of a rose; we are told that the McCoy-Hatfield hostilities had their inception in a squabble over a porker, and likely as not an animal of the razorback variety at that. The McCoys bit thumbs at each other, or "had at it", for forty years, with their dispute intensified by Rose Anne McCoy's love for Jonse Hatfield. Knowledge of the Rosanna-Jonse love affair leads one to speculate on whether or not either or both of the Kentucky principals knew of the Verona tragedy. The Wars of the Roses, we learn, after thirty years of strife ended with a marriage between members of the contending factions. The "Kaintucky" contest, after it had degenerated into a commercial squabble that threatened the Nation's economy, was ended by the intervention of President Harding.[15]

The Sutton-Taylor feud, down Cuero way in southern Texas, a strife which flourished with varying degrees of warmth during the 70's of the last century, died down when John Wesley Hardin was sent up for a sixteen-year stretch at the Huntsville State Penitentiary. Hardin, the Mercutio of the Taylor faction, was both by temperament and physical qualities splendidly equipped for feuding.[16] None of the Taylors, however, was ever inept enough to rush in between Hardin and a Sutton antagonist as does Romeo when Mercutio is fatally stabbed; or if he did, there is no record of the act.

O. Henry very prettily varies this theme of family discord in

15 *The Hatfields and the McCoys*, V, XXVI.
16 *The Life of John Wesley Hardin, As Written by Himself*, p. 81 *et seq.*

"A Technical Error". Here he has Ben Tatum run away with Ella Baynes, Sam Durkee's sweetheart. The Tatums and the Durkees have been feuding for an undisclosed number of years. We will have to presume that their contention had its roots in Kentucky or elsewhere, since at the time events in the story are supposed to occur, palefaces had but recently settled in the Indian Territory. And it is to be noted, likewise, that shortly after the story starts moving, the revenge motif overshadows the feudist theme; this must be so since Ella Baynes is merely a sweetheart and not yet a bona fide member of the Durkee family. Despite this technical difference, Sam Durkee feels compelled to be ruled by the feudist code, a chief tenet of which says that the avenger cannot kill the male-villain while he is in the presence of THE WOMAN – and of course Ben knows that Sam will be governed by the code. Either through frivolity or by design the fleeing Ben ere long swaps raiment with the fickle Ella. In a hotel dining-room in the town of Chandler, Sam detects the cheat and ends the mortal career of Ben with six shots from his Colt automatic. These six shots, we should mention, are a concession to popular tradition, since Sam with his self-loader could just as well have weighed down his antagonist's carcass with double the number of shots he fired. The six discharges presumably represent the intensity of the avenger's contempt for his rival.

Sam can derive satisfaction from having proved to Ella that he is a better man than Ben was, but the quietus the avenger here puts on the offender is not a perfect case of revenge, like the one Poe tells us of in "The Cask of Amontillado". There is ample reason to suppose that Ben never knew what hurt him. It is hardly likely, however, that Sam Durkee would ever let his love for Ella Baynes "illuminate the lives of the two forever", as do Bartley Campbell's Joe Saunders and Mary Brandon; the denouement, if nothing else, would prevent such an unethical attachment.[17]

---

[17] Bartley Campbell, *My Partner*, Act IV.

VIII

A NUECES COUNTRY IDYL

"The king was a terrible old man who wore six-shooters and
spurs, and shouted in such a tremendous voice that the rattlers on
the prairie would run into their holes under the prickly pear."
Thus does O. Henry present "Whispering Ben" O'Donnell, the
cattle king, in "The Princess and the Puma". Whispering Ben of
the strong voice may remind some readers of the non-fictional
Shanghai Pierce, the Rhode Island paradox, who became a noteworthy Texas cattlemen in the period following the Civil War.
Charlie Siringo tells us that the six-foot-four Abel Pierce "had
a voice equal to the foghorn of a river steamboat".[1] As to the
"addition" of "cattle king", we find from the records that Thomas
O'Connor was one of the first cattlemen of Texas to bear that
title. The San Antonio City Directory of 1883-84 lists Thomas
O'Connor, a partner of the banking firm of O'Connor and Sullivan, as the "Texas Cattle King", and states that he was worth
four million dollars. O'Connor had come to Texas from Ireland
in 1834, and was the youngest soldier at San Jacinto. As a land-
owner he was the first to enclose under fence a pasture (of 10,000
acres) in Refugio county; and at his death (October 16, 1887) he
owned 500,000 acres of land, completely surrounded by barbed-
wire fences; O'Connor's estate then was said to be valued at
$4,500,000. The rancher's holdings included land in Refugio, Go-
liad, San Patricio, McMullen, and La Salle counties – the last
county, of course, the site of part of Dull Brothers' acreage, where
young Sydney Porter spent time with Dick Hall. An unusual thing

[1] *Riata and Spurs*, XI, 141.

about O'Connor's marriage was that he and his bride-to-be rode one hundred miles on horseback into San Antonio to have their wedding ceremony performed. Certainly here was a gentleman fit to be a king.[2]

Touching the matter of the *colorado claro* queen, O'Donnell's wife, who had been a Mexican girl from Laredo and who had departed this life before we meet daughter Josefa, such an origin for a cowman's queen as indicated here is not without parallel in pastoral annals. Captain Mifflin Kenedy, who established the Kenedy Pasture Company in 1882, a spread of terrain twenty miles broad and thirty miles long, had, some years prior to this event, married Mrs. Vela de Vidal of Mier, Mexico.[3]

We could wish for more of Whispering Ben, but the author chooses to keep the king in the background and develop instead a pastoral romance of the *As You Like It* order. For this idyl of the Nueces country he brings in Ripley Givens, cowman on the make, and the king's daughter, the brush-country Rosalind, Josefa O'Donnell. As props he uses a Mexican lion or puma, sex not stated, a tomato can, a .38-calibre silver-mounted six-shooter, Givens' Stetson hat, and his unnamed pony, a flea-bitten sorrel maybe, or a red roan. Ripley Givens, encamped for the night at a water-hole on the wooded banks of the Nueces river, spies a puma couching and eager to spring upon the beautiful Josefa as she rests on her hands and knees drinking at the river's brim. The fair damsel, to all seeming, is in imminent danger. The unarmed cowpoke runs forward and dives between the charging lion and the girl. Josefa, however, recognizing the seriousness of the emergency, with a quick eye and a hand fully as fast, sinks a brace of .38 slugs in the head of the rampant beast.

As Givens crawls from under the lion's carcass, it takes him but a minute to see that he is more of a Touchstone than an Orlando. With Rip it is a matter of love discovering a path out of a mess, and this he seeks to do by assuming the role of a clown. If he does a silly thing in pretending that the fierce puma was a camp pet whose life he was trying to save, he has noble precedent

[2]   *Trail Drivers of Texas*, II, 922.
[3]   *Ibid.*, II, 957.

for his curious behavior. Touchstone, as we know, affirms that he kissed the cow's dugs instead of the pretty chap'd hands that milked them; moreover, he recalls wooing a peascod instead of his love, but deftly averts embarrassment by removing the peas and handing the girl two cods and saying, "Wear these for my sake."[4]

At the moment of Rip's debasement, Josefa shows that she has a Rosalind heart. She pretends to go along with Rip's silly fiction for reasons that are too obvious for explanation. In the end of the story, with the aid of Whispering Ben, who reappears for this minor function, we find that Josefa has known all along that the puma was the fierce "Gotch-eared Devil" and not Rip's straying camp kitty.

In *As You Like It* we recall that a lioness comes upon the cruel brother Oliver as he lies sleeping. Orlando, seeing the brother's peril, risks his life to save the fellow (whom he has more reason to hate than to love), and is wounded severely in the arm for his efforts. Orlando also frightens away a green and gilded snake which, if not molested, could have crawled down his brother's throat and choked him.

Some realists might object to this serpent and lioness as unlikely denizens of the forest of Arden; but everyone knows that pumas do range along the Nueces. The improbability in the Texas story is that since pumas rarely carry an attack to man it is not likely that one would harm Josefa.

Both Josefa and Rosalind, to achieve their honorable ends, deceive the men they love. Josefa does not let on that she knows the identity of the Gotch-eared Devil; she has her reasons for telling Rip, "How terrible it would be to meet a really wild lion!" And Rosalind, more delicately drawn and set out on a much wider canvas, feigning, in the guise of the boy Ganimede, to cure Orlando of his love, makes him woo her as Rosalind. Josefa is a *carté visité* protagonist, but entrancing nevertheless, if only faintly sketched.

As You Like It furnished inspiration for another character of

[4] *As You Like It*, II, iv.

the author's. He says of Dry Valley Johnson (in the story, "The Indian Summer of Dry Valley Johnson"): "He was but a melancholy Jaques of the forest with a ruder philosophy, lacking the bitter-sweet flavor of experience that tempered the veteran years of the rugged ranger of Arden."

IX

LAW OFFICERS, FEARFUL AND FEARLESS

O. Henry writes facetiously of the "human Texas mind" as a singular kind of governing faculty that is the peculiar property of inhabitants of the Lone Star State. Deputy marshal Buck Caperton in "The Lonesome Road" is presented to the reader as a character embodying such a mentality. Tall of stature, bronzed by the summer sun, and fittingly decorated with jingling spurs and "forty-fives", Caperton with his fearlessness and determination satisfies the commonly accepted idea of a Western officer of the law. Moreover, Caperton shows no interest whatever in woman, a further qualification of a criminologist, as Dr. Watson tells us on the authority of Sherlock Holmes.[1] The marshal does have a trivial weakness, but this distinguishes rather than detracts from his character: he has a passion for corn-husk cigarettes, even though he cannot roll them.

The author-narrator, an old friend of the officer, makes a cigarette for him and then listens as Buck tells how marriage has metamorphosed his former partner Perry Roundtree from a top-hand at "stirring up the echoes" to a docile stay-at-home husband all "corrupted and Willie-ized", a "frivolous fraction of a man". Roundtree, as the marshal's account has it, after many pleas from Caperton, agrees to indulge in "one more rip-roaring razoo" with his old buddy. He accompanies Caperton to a former haunt of theirs, the back room of the Gray Mule Saloon, to turn himself loose till half-past six. When the men stop at the bar, Caperton is shocked to hear his long-time pal name sarsaparilla as his drink,

[1] *A Scandal in Bohemia*, p. 3.

and is dumbfounded when the man elects to play checkers instead of bucking the tiger. Soon the two sit down to play. Perry immediately becomes engrossed in the game and Buck reluctantly yields to humor his friend is his "debauch". Every once in a while, as they play, Perry remarks that he must be home by seven.

At half-past six or thereabouts an event happens that gives the lie to Buck's inferences about his old side-kick's transformation. The Trimble outfit – all ten of them – the worst gang of desperadoes in Texas – begin to shoot up the Gray Mule barroom. Buck, disturbed, rises to look and see what is going on; but Perry, declaring again that he must be home by seven, is unmindful of the "nonsense" and plays on. After another game, he gets up from the table and says that he must hurry home. As he makes ready to open the door into the barroom, Caperton steps in front of him to block his way.

Married man . . ., I know you was christened a fool the minute the preacher tangled you up, but don't you never sometimes think one little think on a human basis? There's ten of that gang in there, and they're pizen with whiskey and desire for murder. They'll drink you up like a bottle of booze before you get halfway to the door. . . . Sit down and wait till we have some chance to get out without being carried in baskets.

The fear motif is emphasized rather playfully when Perry insists again that he has "got to be home by seven". This husband who is apparently afraid to disobey his wife's injunction about returning home at the designated time shows an utter lack of fear of the most desperate and villainous of men, "holy terrors" who are full of liquor and dead-set to kill. With the aid of table legs and a Winchester which Buck grabs from a Trimble, the two friends make their way safely through the barroom.

At home, Perry's wife Mariana greets her beloved with a "kind of look" and a long breath, and the reproachful remark, "You're late, Perry."

The look which the little woman gives Perry, a sign of wifely concern for her husband, proves to Buck Caperton that he has been nourishing a restricted idea of a Texas peace officer. Witty, hardy, courageous, sharp-eyed, and as "nervy as they come", he sees now that his iron-man and Benedick image has been an illusion. It is this "kind of look", which Buck cannot describe that convinces him that he, and not his ex-ranger colleague who bears the conjugal yoke, has been the fool of the game.

Ranger Lieutenant Sandridge appears to be fearless enough to perform the duties of an officer, but he obviously is not sufficiently wary in his search for offenders, if we are to judge by the way he goes after the Cisco Kid; the law-officer's lack of circumspection is a tragic flaw in his make-up; in addition, he shows a weakness that Buck Caperton would have been ashamed to entertain: he falls in love – falls a victim to the wiles of a Mexican señorita who is not exactly "out of the top drawer".[2] Buck Caperton, as a law officer, it must be admitted, is on more solid ground in his distaste for affairs of the heart. Although Sandridge has the size and looks and ostensible bravery of a typical Texas Ranger of the period, he lacks skill in the science of deduction. He attracts the fickle Tonia simply because he is blond and big; and he seeks to bind her fascination for him through the medium of the six-strand plait.[3] Caperton, a witty, more gifted man than Sandridge, we feel could have become a real Benedick had a Beatrice fortuned to encounter him. A man who could talk to Perry Roundtree the way Buck Caperton does could hold his own even with a Katherine, or any other barbed-tongue shrew.

Well, then, you poor, contaminated adjunct of a sprinklingpot and degraded household pet, what did you go and do it for? Look at you, all decent and unriotous, and only fit to sit on juries and mend the wood-house door. You was a man once. I have hostility for all such acts.[4]

We think that all of Sandridge meets our eye when he first appears – a plain, able, and determined man – and we continue to think so until we perceive how deftly the Cisco Kid enmeshes him in his snare and makes him snuff out the life of the capricious little humming bird, Tonia Perez.[5] Such an ignominy is no part of the business of a hero.

[2] "The Caballero's Way", *Works*, I, 204-211.
[3] *Ibid.*, 206.
[4] "The Lonesome Road", *Works*, I, 545.
[5] "The Caballero's Way", *ibid.*, 211.

Another Buck who attracts our attention is Marshal Buck Patterson of "The Reformation of Calliope". This second Buck is depicted as an intrepid but tolerant kind of officer who understands the will of a community that is opposed to a "too strict enforcement of the law". Town badman Catesby, however, finally exhausts the marshal's patience with his "rip-roarous shoot-'em up" behavior, and invites a conflict with the officer. Catesby, paradoxically we may say, but like other of O. Henry's noisy desperadoes, is fearless and accurate with his pistols. In a showdown with Patterson he knocks the officer out by "barking" him; the marshal does not come to until the riotous Calliope's old mother appears before him as she enters the depot from an incoming train. When the prostrate Patterson regains consciousness, he sees Catesby hiding his guilt from his mother by masquerading as marshal. The indulgent officer approves of the cheat as a measure to correct the splenetic Calliope's singular waywardness. The practice of such philosophy of criminal reform would today qualify Patterson for a warden's job in a department of corrections.

Ranger Lieutenant Bob Buckley in "An Afternoon Miracle" is a study of an officer whose willing mind is in conflict with a physical weakness. As the story opens, Bob and his three compadres, Bronco Leathers, the Nueces Kid, and a misguided Eastern man are in the border town of Laredo to curb the outlandish behavior of Mexican badman Leandro García. For a long time Bob has successfully concealed his fear from his companions by using his authority as head officer to throw himself alone into all scraps which the detachment has been ordered to quell. In these contests he always "gave away weight", as the Eastern man's boxing term described the leader's method. García sneaks across the Rio Grande in the guise of an old female faggot vender and, taking advantage of his "masquerootin'", is able to inflict a wound in the shoulder of Bud Dawson, barkeeper of the Top Notch Saloon. In accord with the tenets of his philosophy, when Dawson tells him that García carries only two sixes and a knife, Buckley cuts his armament down to his two revolvers and his "Bowie" and starts out for the Mexican quarter on his Quixotic pursuit of the elusive bandit.

Fate brings Buckley face to face with Alvarita, a fearless snake charmer without equal in her profession, and fittingly denominated "Queen of the Serpent Tribe". Alvarita's private railroad car is side-tracked at a little 'dobe depot in the Mexican section because of the failure of a Mexican Central train to make connection with the I. & G. N. train for Santone. Precisely at the time when Buckley reaches this "ragged edge" of the town, Alvarita is out in search of her great eleven-foot Asian python, Kuku, who has escaped from his box in the car. It is somewhat of a paradox that this girl Alvarita, who looks Spanish — more specifically, Andalusian or Basque — and exhibits such mastery in the serpent world, should call an *arroyo* a *crick*, have a picture of Abraham Lincoln in her car-home, and call Gallipolis her home instead of Seville. It is paradoxical, likewise, that a Ranger lieutenant should entertain a dread of any living thing; but he does, and as he sets out for García he feels the cold sweat on his brow and "the old, shameful, dreaded sinking of his heart". He is in this pitiful condition when he runs smack on to Alvarita. "The Miracle" is a story of a man and his sentience of fear. But unlike Roderick Usher, who is miserably wrought up by the notion that he will ultimately perish in a struggle with his fear, Bob Buckley wilfully encounters situations in which he tries vigorously to shuffle off the painful emotion that sickens him.[6] Tom Lea's Luis Bello is more like Buckley: the dread that encompasses Bello in his moment of triumph at Cuenca leaves him and goes out to the spectators, who then experience a great terror for the matador's safety.[7]

Kuku the python lies joyfully in his concealment and watches his mistress with the full knowledge that if retaken he will be powerless in bold hands; we see Alvarita, too, showing her bravery as García comes walking up the slope, telling the Gallipol*ees* girl that he will not "hurty" her.

"You bet you won't", she replies. "But don't you think you had better move on?"

At a critical moment, Bob Buckley approaches the Mexican

---

6   Edgar Allan Poe, *The Fall of the House of Usher*, I, 161.
7   Tom Lea, *The Brave Bulls*, XVIII, 261.

and seeing the latter with his holsters empty, in conformity with his code, he unbuckles and lets his pair of sixes fall to the ground.

As the ranger advances toward García, barehanded, fear again takes him in its clutches: his throat becomes dry, his heart throbs violently, and his stomach sickens. While in this state of agitation, he looks upward and his glance becomes riveted for a second on a pair of dark, soft, and tender eyes. The sentience of fear, by the magic of this communion, is transferred from the failing heart of the man to the bold heart of the girl. Animated now by a courage he had never known, Buckley, still empty-handed, delivers a knockout punch on the Latin's jaw; he administers the blow with a suddenness that sends the badman down with a knife useless in his hand.

Thus concludes a neat little story of how a ranger, a singularity among his kind, gains courage from the heart of a bold girl – and perhaps wins the girl herself – who is now transformed into a timid, womanly, admirable creature, a charmer of men instead of reptiles, and so delicately shy that she cries "Ooh" and trembles at the sight of a caterpillar.

X

COUNTERFEIT WOMEN, HOAXES, AND NOBLE SAVAGES

In "The Marquis and Miss Sally" the reader finds two old literary devices in new attire, devices that are moldy with antiquity: we refer to the practical joke or hoax and the woman in disguise. Sally Bascom's cowman father is robbed of his entire herd and killed by Indian cattle-thieves on the same day that the Marquis of Borodale becomes a *felo de se* when he finds himself a ruined man at his home in Regent's Square, London. As a consequence of this brace of catastrophes, the Marquis's only son, a solid and prosperous rancher of the Texas Panhandle, and Sally Bascom find themselves at the same time hitting-up the manager of Diamond Cross for jobs as cow-hands. Sally Bascom is disguised as a boy, and, of course, although pretty enough for a heroine of romance, as it develops later on, is not recognized as a female by her employer, nor by any of the riding pokes who certainly must have ears moderately well attuned to the rustle of a skirt. The real marquis soon "gets wise" to her identity, as one might expect, because it is necessary for the progress of the scene that he do so. The author, however, has committed no indiscretion in ordering his narrative in this manner, since neither Orlando nor the banished Duke nor the melancholy Jaques has the remotest notion in the world of the real gender of the fair Rosalind when the disguised girl makes her entry into the Arden forest; this is the situation despite the fact that any audience whoever saw Julia Marlowe, or Edith Wynne Mattheson, or Madame Helena Modjeska fitted out for a jaunt in the romantic wildwood could detect the cheat the very moment the rise of the curtain reveals the woodland scene.[1]

O. Henry is certainly on solid, realistic ground when he has Sally Bascom do her job of holding the herd during the cuttings without any but the true Marquis discovering that she is a counterfeit woman. In the province of romance a woman can disguise herself as a man without fear of detection, because such is the manner of life in the realm of fancy. The imagination, we feel, can devise the most fantastic of situations; but often in real life we can find the equal to the wild imaginings of the fictionist. Trail-driver Samuel Dunn Houston shows that a girl can pose as a man, do a man's work in a cow camp, and keep her true sex hidden from those she works among. She may become a bit dirty in the process, but she can apparently sustain the part handsomely enough if she has the will to do so.

Houston tells of how he hired a "kid of a boy" in Clayton, New Mexico, and put him with his horses to take the place of the "rustler", whom he transferred to a job with the cows.

The kid would get up [on] the darkest stormy nights and stay with the cattle until the storm was over. He was good natured, very modest, didn't use any cuss words or tobacco, and was always pleasant. His name was Willie Mathews. He was nineteen years old and he weighed one hundred and twenty-five pounds. His home was in Caldwell, Kansas, and I was so pleased with him that I wished many times that I could find two or three more like him.[2]

When Houston's band of drovers reached Hugo, Colorado, Willie Mathews, claiming to be homesick, asked for and gained the boss's consent to quit the camp and go home. At sundown on the very day of her departure, her camp waddies were astonished to see an attractive woman approaching camp as they lolled round the wagon eating supper. Shortly thereafter, all the hands were dumbfounded to discover that the Willie Mathews they had known was a girl. She explained to the astonished Houston that as the

---

[1]   Anyone who desires further knowledge about these celebrated late nineteenth- and early twentieth-century players should consult the later volumes of Odell's *The History of the New York Stage*.

[2]   *The Trail Drivers of Texas*, I, 71, 76, 77.

daughter of an old Texas trail-driver she had joined his outfit to see at first-hand what life was in a cow-camp.

"I suppose she was the only girl that ever made such a trip as that", concludes Houston. "She was a perfect lady." [3]

A deception such as that practiced by Willie Mathews is not hard to understand when we bear in mind that it took an astute detective of the calibre of Ulysses to find out the false pose of Achilles when that noble Grecian knight elected to hide himself among women.[4]

Sally Bascom proves to be a perfect lady too. We recall that O. Henry shows her at first to be "a pleasant fellow, always a little reserved and taking no part in the rough camp frolics". And of course she cannot do these because of the very nature of some of those pranks. Her skill with the rope and in the branding pen undoubtedly makes her assumption of the masculine rôle credible to every one – that is, to every one but the true Marquis.

When cowpoke Phonograph Davis sets up the mock-wedding of "Miss Sally" and the Marquis, he is merely planning a joke commonly practiced in cow camps. He of course does not know that the person he calls a marquis is really Sally Bascom, nor that a real marquis is the camp cook. "Miss Sally", as the author explains, is a generic term for cow-country cooks. A county judge out campaigning happens on the scene, and the actual marquis contrives to have an "honest-to-goodness" wedding performed.

As to the practical joke, or hoax, that forms a good part of the body of the story, George W. Harris has shown us in one of his Sut Lovingood yarns how great a source of hilarity a wedding can be. We have in mind the yarn about Sut breaking up Sicily Burns' wedding with old Sock, the black and white bull.[5] There's levelled malice in Sut's action, it must be conceded, but malice is the motivating force in almost all of Sut's violent action. Sut schemes all of his pranks because of this quirk in his nature.

---

[3] *Ibid.*
[4] Thetis, knowing that her son was fated to perish before Troy, sent him to the court of King Lycomedes of Scyrus; here his mother induced him to dress as a woman and hide himself among the daughters of the king. Charles Mills Gayley, *The Classic Myths*, XXII, 279, 280.
[5] "Sicily Burns' Wedding", *Sut Lovingood's Yarns*, pp. 86-97.

Actor James H. Wallick, as we have seen, found a marriage on horseback an attractive feature for his melodrama, *The Cattle King*.

Cowhands were naturally given to the gentle art of perpetrating hoaxes, or, we could more fittingly say, to the pastime of *selling* the gullible. Gus Black tells how he "fooled" Governor Bush of Wyoming. On an occasion when Black was delivering a herd of stocker cattle for John W. Lytle, in order to have a little fun he fastened "a couple of longhorns which had slipped from the head of a [grown] cow onto the head of a dogie yearling which ran along with the drags". Black bet the governor $200 that the animal was just a yearling. The governor, judging the brute by the length of his horns, contended that he was a four-year-old. The reader can imagine the magistrate's chagrin when he saw the horns removed to reveal the tender age of the little bovine critter.[6]

Can an aborigine be removed from his tribal environment, dressed in the habiliments of the paleface, educated in football and literature in an Anglo-Saxon college, and as a result cleanse from his mind, wholly and forever, the remembrance of dog-feasts, dingy squaws, and ghost dances? O. Henry, in the person of John Tom Little Bear (in "The Atavism of John Tom Little Bear"), shows that a redskin, subjected to the impulses of such factors as those hinted at above, will revert to type when precipitated suddenly into a crisis.

As the story has it, John Tom Little Bear joins fakir Jefferson Peters in a scheme to remove surplus dollars from the purses of gullible Kansas citizens. The two men plan to perform this art chiefly through the sale of a magic soap, valuable for the removal of grease spots, and an Indian herb remedy, called Sum-wah-tah, a kind of health-giving tonic. The operation gets under way and proceeds with the success that usually rewards the efforts which Mr. Jefferson Peters makes for the removal of idle dollars from the pockets of the unsuspecting populace. One evening as Little

Bear sits cooking a stew in his tent he is assaulted by a "fresh, cheeky" kid with a pellet-gun. "Cowardly redskin", says the kid. ... "Dare to burn me at the stake..." Exhibiting a quantity of cheek himself, Little Bear starts up, grabs, and questions his assailant as to his motives for the attack. The kid softens when questioned, with the result that Little Bear and Peters soon have him employed as an assistant in their vending routine. The two grafters soon find that the brassy kid has much more to him than they at first think he has, and when Peters finds his mother and she comes on the scene, Little Bear, now deeply attached to the youngster, begins to manifest all the symptoms of a paleface in love.

"Jeff, for how many ponies do you think I could buy Mrs. Conyers?" (Mrs. Conyers is of course the young boy's mother.) Little Bear goes on a bit later to explain what the white man has done to him by sending him to college. "You've made me a Cherokee Moses. You've taught me to hate the wigwams and love the white man's ways. I can look over into the promised land and see Mrs. Conyers, but my place is on the reservation."[7]

While Little Bear, in his dumps, is solacing himself with the white man's resource when in this condition, fire-water that is, the villain paleface, Mrs. Conyer's no-account husband, comes suddenly into town, kidnaps, and runs away with the child.

Here is a crisis that transforms Mr. J. T. Little Bear, alumnus of the class of '91, into the "original proposition in bear's claws and copper color". After a fifteen-mile run the Indian overtakes the villain, retrieves the child, and returns with the abductor's scalp hanging from his belt. No broken twigs crack under this aborigine's feet as he runs in pursuit; nor does he, like Chingachgook, turn a stream out of its course to find the moccasin tracks of the pursued.[8] John Tom's failure to display a knowledge of these particular facets of woodcraft, as a Cooper Indian might do when tracking a fugitive, can be accounted for partly because the

---

[7] "The Atavism of John Tom Little Bear", *Works*, II, 964.
[8] Mark Twain, "Fenimore Cooper's Literary Offences", *Literary Essays*, pp. 85 ff.

kidnapper flees with his victim in a buggy; and partly, too, because there may have been no trees along the route the scoundrel follows as he flees. Little Bear simply sees the absconding critter with the child in his custody and takes off in pursuit.

On the morning after the rescue, the Noble Savage wakes up with the 19th century back in his eyes.

"What was it?" he asks Jeff; and Jeff explains, "Heap firewater."

John looks about a little, and soon finds himself.

"Combined", says he presently, "with the interesting little physiological shake-up known as reversion to type. I remember now. Have they gone yet?"

At this point we cannot but recall the behavior of Fenimore Cooper's Hard Heart on a memorable occasion. At the time referred to this chieftain is confronted with the problem of dismissing from his life a beautiful woman who certainly must have been impressed with the skillful quietus he had shortly before inflicted on the dirty dog Mahtoree. Captain Middleton, who has shortly before recaptured his kidnapped wife Inez, is fearful lest the great Pawnee cast a wistful eye on the pretty Spanish señora. And we cannot blame him for entertaining such a suspicion. He, unlike Natty Bumppo, has such a limited knowledge of Indians that he could hardly be expected to make the proper distinction between a "dirty dog" and a "noble savage". So there is sufficient reason for the young artillery officer's misgiving. The great Loup, as the reader of the novel knows, is nobility personified.[9] At the end of a Homeric oration in which he extols the virtues of his own warrior nation and those of such Big Knives as Captain Middleton and his associates, Hard-Heart eases off into a panegyric of Mrs. Middleton: he declares that she "no doubt was the most obedient, the meekest, the loveliest of them all".[10] John Tom Little Bear, with his pale-face college training, could not have done any better for himself than the Pawnee leader does. Hard-Heart does make one mistake, albeit a natural one for a Pawnee

---

[9]   James Fenimore Cooper, *The Prairie, passim.*
[10]   *Ibid.*, XXXIII, 431.

Loup: he presumes that the Captain has other wives than Inez. But certainly the chief's intentions towards Inez de Certavallos Middleton are of the most honorable sort. Like Little Bear, who says that his place is on the reservation, Hard-Heart believes that his is in the American desert chasing the wild buffalo.

XI

A MELANGE OF RECHERCHÉ SPECIALTIES

Charles Dickens was perhaps the most influential of the writers who popularized low-life characters in England in the nineteenth century; the "cheeky" young pickpocket of *Oliver Twist*, the "Artful Dodger", is one of the best known creations in English fiction. Bret Harte, somewhat later than the English novelist, demonstrated the possibilities of similar material in his shorter compositions here in America. Following the Civil War, with the growth and extension of the railroads over the continent, the tramp or hobo, the modern version of the older vagabond, became a fixture on the American scene. The tramp as a comic character became as popular on the stage in O. Henry's time as the clown had been in Shakespeare's days. One of actor Sol Smith Russell's best personations was that of a "drunken, shabby tramp". Russell, who had begun his career as a platform "protean" or "rapid change artist", with the comic vagrant as one of his quick changes, later carried the creation about with him as an added attraction to his homespun drama, *Edgewood Folks*.[1] So popular indeed did his "specialty" sketch of the tramp become that he eventually was to find the assumption as hard to get rid of as Frank Mayo did his Davy Crockett, or James O'Neill his Monte Cristo.

With this low-life character enjoying the wide vogue that he did, it is with little wonder that we find William Sydney Porter giving his readers a perfectly fresh, individualistic conception of this member of the leisure class in the person of Whistling Dick in a story that appeared in *McClure's Magazine* in December,

---

[1] San Antonio *Light* (November 3, 1882).

1899.[2] The story referred to is Porter's first under the pseudonym of O. Henry. Whistling Dick travels in or under boxcars, speaks like a Bowery tough, hates work, loves rest, but has pride (professional and other) and a sense of honor hardly noticeable in the general run of the hoboes met with on the stage, or seen at the back door, or found walking down railroad tracks. Dick is portrayed as having the same horror of cleanliness as that shown in the face of Phil May's figure of the vagabond in the Pears' soap advertisement in *Munsey's Magazine* at the turn of the century. The "ad" shows this eccentric creature reading in great amazement a startling announcement set forth in large letters before him: "Whilst There's Life There's SOAP."[3]

Dick has unquestionable musical talent. As a top-grade whistler, his range extends from *Der Freishütz* (possibly an air from this work, or perhaps a phrase or so from an overture) to the intermezzo from *Cavalleria Rusticana*. Dick's ability to whistle an air from the Weber opera better than policeman "Big Fritz" can himself induces the officer to give the genial wanderer the "pest tip you efer had". Later, too, the mistress of Bellemeade is impressed with the way Dick would blow the spirit of Mascagni into the *Cavalleria* intermezzo.

Many readers of the story at the time of its publication must have recognised Big Fritz as a contemporary of police "rounder", John Mishler (in the comedy *One of the Finest*) and Captain Mishler (in the sequel, the play *Captain Mishler*), both rôles the assumptions of the talented German dialect comedian, Gus Williams.[4] To give his parts a wider appeal, Williams invariably adorned them with interpolations of songs and recitations.

---

[2]   "Whistling Dick's Christmas Stocking", *Mc Clure's Magazine*, XIV, 138 (November, 1899-April, 1900).
[3]   Advertising Section, *Munsey's Magazine*, XXVIII, No. 1 (October, 1902). The writer recalls also another Phil May cartoon depicting a tramp, with satisfaction plainly visible in his countenance, as he makes his way along the rails. Beside the sketch is the notation: "Twenty years ago, I used Pears' soap. Since then I have used no other."
[4]   Gus Williams was a native of the part of New York known as Dutchtown. He began his career in vaudeville at Tony Pastor's, gaining prominence first with his portrayal of J. Adolph Dinkel in *Our German Senator* at Haverly's Fourteenth Street Theatre, January 5, 1882. Odell, XI, 170. *One of the*

Dick follows the advice of Fritz, leaves the city, and heads down the river into the sugar country. After some time, as he travels along on the river road, a planter with his wife and young daughter pass him in their double surrey behind a brace of stylish greys. As the vehicle rolls by, the girl, "Ther bloomin' little skeezicks", as Dick calls her, cries out, "Mer-ry Christ-mas!" Dick is touched by the greeting, although at a loss as to what to make of it. Presently he finds a woman's silk stocking that has dropped from the carriage. He picks up the stocking and proceeds on his course until after a while he finds himself in the camp of an old acquaintance, hobo Boston Harry. Harry is somewhat of a paradox himself, what with his parlor manners, his smooth-shaven face, and academic diction. Dick observes that Harry, as usual, is "chewing the stuffing out of the dictionary", as the latter introduces the newcomer to the other vagrants round the camp-fire. Harry soon reveals to Dick his plan of setting fire to the sugar-cane patch and robbing the very planter who has passed Dick on his way back home from a New Orleans bank with money to pay his farm hands. The high-level education of the Boston wanderer may account for his ambition to rise above the mediocrity of petty-thievery to mastermind such a large scale operation as robbing the planter of his payroll cash. We are informed that he has had success in confidence games.

Dick avows that he is a bum, pure and simple, and will not join in the nefarious scheme. (He declines the invitation before he discovers the identity of the intended victims, a display of goodness which is a point in his favor.) Harry thereupon reveals a side of his nature that would seem to remove him from the realm of tramphood: he covers the dissenter with a short revolver, and declares, "The end of the brick pile is your limit. You go two inches beyond that and I'll have to shoot."

At this point in the story some readers might question the likelihood of having Dick find close by a roundish stone to fit into the toe of the stocking to make a kind of "meteorite" the

---

Finest opened for a long run on June 19, 1882. *Ibid.*, 472. *Captain Mishler* was performed for the first time at Haverly's Comedy Theatre on May 26, 1884. *Ibid.*, XII, 341.

clever being has in mind. The stone seems to be just the size and conformation to satisfy the need. Stones of any kind are scarce articles along the banks of the Mississippi below New Orleans. One can surmise that the object had originally been part of a building ornament and was later discarded with the bricks that formed the pile in the camp lot. It may be equally surprising to others to note that the musical bum is able to catapult the stocking-missile a full seventy-five yards with the accuracy of an Olympic hammer-thrower. Riding on the rods, as itinerants of the leisure class so often see the need of doing, has a tendency to cramp rather than make supple the extensor muscles of the arms. The bracing outdoor air, however, imparts a vigor to the physique that people of sedentary habits have but a bowing acquaintance with. It is no extraordinary feat for Dick to get his message through.

The planter heeds the warning, apprehends the villains, and tries to reward the informant for his beneficial act. But Whistling Dick, a tramp by nature, is unable to sustain the role of hero. His professional pride urges him to revert to type, just as surely as Black Eagle feels the urge to shed his eagle plumage for that of a chicken.[5] The Whistler's declaration to Boston Harry, that "burglary is no good", may in a way indicate a sense of moral values, but the man's dislike of water for external use and his fear of the ogre of Labor are more "in character".

Shakespeare's Christopher Sly, a "rogue", or tramp of sorts of earlier days, is of a mold utterly different from that in which Whistling Dick was cast. We recall how, in the Induction of *The Taming of the Shrew*, a lord returning from a hunt finds Sly in a drunken sleep, like a dead swine, before an ale-house door. The lord bets his huntsmen that Sly will entirely forget his identity if carried up and put in his lordship's fairest chamber, and then dressed in scented clothes, with rings on his fingers, and treated to a sumptuous meal of delicate viands. Sly is likewise to be most agreeably attended by solicitous servants.[6] He has somewhat of a struggle with himself when subjected to the trial but in a short

[5] "The Passing of Black Eagle", *Works*, I, 438.
[6] William Shakespeare, *The Taming of the Shrew*, Induction.

while overcomes his "strange lunacy", and declares himself to be
a man of noble birth.

Sly. By th' Mass, I think I am a Lord indeed.

.   .   .   .

Where is my wife? [7]

Twenty caged nightingales, sweet music, gay and costly apparel,
draughts of sack, a promise of gaily harnessed horses, wanton
pictures, and a distressed though counterfeit wife who has longed
for her husband's return to his bed – all lures that tug hard at the
doubtful mind – help carry the jest with Sly. In this way the lord
proves his point. Whistling Dick of course encounters no such en-
ticements. To him the planter makes a "solid" business-like appeal. A position of trust is promised Dick at once, with the chance
of advancement suited to his powers later on. A promise of this
sort must have seemed vague to a man who looks on life as one
good handout after another. The portable bathtub, the washstand
and flowered bowl, factors that might have turned Sly, are frightening to the Whistler. And there too is the unwholesome suggestion of the bed with its snowy pillows and sheets. Dick is to his
manner of life born. If we believe that this musically-bent vagrant
would have been a farm-manager or vaudeville player under other
and more propitious circumstances, we may explain him by saying
that Fortune was just too late in taking away the barricade she
had set up between him and his destiny.

One is likewise amused to observe in this matter of the behavior of beggars that editor Lewis Theobald comments on Sly's
penchant for the misuse of words in terms reminiscent of Dick's
observation about Boston Harry's "Chewin' de stuffin' out'n de
dictionary". Says Theobald: "Sly, as an ignorant Fellow, is pur-
posely made to aim at Languages out of his knowledge, and knock
the Words out of Joint." [8]

Whistling Dick flees from the poppied-warmth of the big-house
boudoir and makes his way over to the river. His piccolo-notes
startle a little brown-breasted bird that sits on a dogwood sapling
piping its praises of the December morning dew. This touch of

7   *Ibid.*
8   *Ibid.*

the neo-pathetic fallacy puts us in mind of a similar scene in Bret Harte. As Jack Hamlin rides deeper into the dim woods on his trusty gray mount he presently bursts into song, a sentimental plaint about his "Nelly's grave".

"A sparrow-hawk, fresh from his sixth victim possibly recognizing in Mr. Hamlin a kindred spirit, stared at him in surprise, and was fain to confess the superiority of man. With a superior predatory capacity *he* couldn't sing." [9]

There is much in the behavior and career of the hobo Chicken Ruggles that suggests a kinship with Dickens' Noah Claypole, a despicable underworld creature in *Oliver Twist*. Chicken, a man of several aliases, graces the pages of "The Passing of Black Eagle". Of course Ruggles is ostensibly a tramp, but that does not mean that he can be ruled out as a "beat" or opportunist. He seems to be the kind of man who will grab Opportunity by the forelook when he meets him face to face, but is too deeply imbued with tramp philosophy to make use of his chance when he has it. We are told of Ruggles, when he is presented to us, that his first essay as a practitioner of the "kinchin lay",[10] the snatching of a bottle of peptonized milk from a baby in his buggy, had landed the hobo in jail for thirty days. The baby's cries had attracted an officer of the law. When Dickens' Claypole arrives in London, he soon meets head-crook Fagin in the master's hangout in the east of the city. Fagin suggests to the prospective convert the snatching of reticules from old women as a suitable employment for a man of his capacity. The prospect, however, with more foresight than Ruggles, concludes that the "hollering" of a lady could result in his arrest. Besides making a noise, the assaulted victim, he feared, might scratch him. Ruggles in his second exploit in the kinchin field is successful. And in this second instance, too, he shows the tact of a veteran. With his last five cents he buys a youngster a bag of chocolate creams, a kind of candy for which the child has professed a liking. In this way he gains the confidence of his intended victim. The Chicken then easily

---

[9]   Bret Harte, *Brown of Calaveras*, I, 68.
[10]   *The Shorter Oxford Dictionary* defines *kinchin lay* "as the practice of stealing money from children sent on errands".

takes from the child the dollar his mother has given him to buy ten cents' worth of paregoric with. The author tells us that Ruggles quits the market with a profit of 1,700 per cent on his invested capital. We are reminded that Claypole, by contrast, on his first venture on the kinchin lay, picks up three pint pots, a milk can, six shillings, nine pence halfpenny. Claypole in a sense, although not percentage wise, does better on his initial foray than Ruggles.

Both of these beats can operate better with their stomachs warmed with ardent spirits. A small brown jug of whisky does for Ruggles what a pot of porter does for Noah Claypole. His confidence established with porter, Claypole feels he could be "the captain of some band and have the whopping of 'em. ... That would suit me, if there was good profit." [11] Claypole, alias Morris Bolter, joins Fagin's gang of thieves and has to be satisfied with a rather modest role in the organization; Chicken Ruggles, alias Captain Montressor, alias Piggy, alias Black Eagle, falls in with a band of Texas outlaws, and actually achieves leadership of the gang. Although he proves to be unequipped for the exacting demands of his position, he does nevertheless talk his way up to head boss. Piggy, on whom the Mexicans have at this point conferred the sobriquet of Black Eagle, declares himself in this manner:

Wat's de use of chasin' little red cowses and hosses 'round for t'ousands of miles? Dere ain't nuttin' in it. ... You know what I'd do if I was main finger of dis bunch? I'd stick up a train. I'd blow de express car and make hard dollars where you guys get wind. [12]

Bud King, the bandit leader, gives in to the urgings of his men and allows Black Eagle to direct them in the holding-up of a train. He does so, but not without misgivings. After noting that the Eagle "ain't never been smoked yet", he adds that the fellow is all right "for skearin' greaser kids..."; he's the finest canned oyster buccaneer and cheese pirate that ever was...". Similarly, Charlie Bates of the Fagin company analyzes Noah Claypole:

The cutting away when there's anything wrong and the eating all the wittles when there's everything right; that's his branch. [13]

[11]   Charles Dickens, *The Adventures of Oliver Twist*, XLII, 262.
[12]   "The Passing of Black Eagle", *Works*, I, 436.
[13]   Charles Dickens, *op. cit.*, XLIII, 271.

Neither Ruggles nor Claypole is above playing false to his comrades when put to the test. Claypole is the more despicable of the two, one may say; he is a "snitcher" as a matter of principle. He would just as readily betray Fagin as Nancy. Ruggles fails in the pinch simply because he is instinctively a tramp, and the smell of excelsior in a boxcar of the train he is to rob metamorphoses him from spurious leader back into a knight of the road.[14]

Curly the tramp, in "The Higher Abdication", we shall dismiss with a few words. Curly adopts the profession of vagrant by the force of circumstance. Brought by chance again to the scene of his origin, he bears all the earmarks of a veteran member of the calling he seems to have adopted: he has a passion for whisky, an overfondness for filthy attire, and a strong distaste for work. But when Ranse Truesdell learns by particular indications that the "maverick" he has befriended is the missing Truesdell heir, and, as a consequence, tests him to see if he is a real, "red-blooded" man, we find that the dirt, the laziness, and fondness for drink are but the veneer of environment. By the strength of his blood, Curly sheds his cocoon and regains his place as old Kiowa Truesdell's rightful heir. His masquerade is so superficial that his transformation is effected almost by the use of soap and towel and a dip into the water of the charco.

As for Ranse himself, the agent of the reclamation, like Ross Hargis in "Hygeia at the Solito" who loves any man that can lick him, he is an apostle of the strenuous life. Teddy Roosevelt could have been his inspiration. The tough fibre and endurance of clean living enable him to "do Curly in" with the awkward and potent blows of his fists. By this process, Curly is transformed into his proper self; and Ranse smiles to know that he has been the instrument in bringing about the wholesome change.

---

[14] An International and Great Northern Railroad time-table in the San Antonio *Express* (August 29, 1884), shows that a mixed train left Laredo daily at 3 P. M. for San Antonio. A mixed train carried both freight and passenger cars.

XII

BADMEN

Prototypes of the characters of O. Henry's Texas *badman* stories can be found among men who lived at the time about which the author writes. These creatures of fancy, more moderate in action than their counterparts in the flesh, he projects within a region of definite bounds, making ample use of background material to add reality to character and incident.

The area that furnishes the settings for the *badman* stories is made up chiefly of the *brasada* or chaparral region along the Rio Grande. In the 70's and 80's this space stretched from King Fisher's Pendencia Creek Ranch near Eagle Pass to the Laguna Madre near Brownsville. It embraced what was then known as the Nueces Strip and was bounded on the south by the Bravo del Norte and the narrow ribbon of no-man's land called the Zona Libre.[1] To the northeast it extended to the Sutton-Taylor feud grounds in and about Cuero; and its northern terminus was the Alamo Plaza at Santone. For the most part it was then, as indeed it is now, a semi-arid tableland of fertile sandy loam, with immense flats of curly mesquite grass and prickly pear.

In "The Caballero's Way" O. Henry calls a pear flat the devil's pincushion, and says that a ride through such an area is more weird and lonesome than the journey of an Amazonian explorer. He further observes of this species of cactus:

This demon plant wraps itself a thousand times about what look to be open and inviting paths, only to lure the rider into blind and im-

---

[1] In the Houston *Weekly Telegraph* (February 3, 1870), the Zona Libre is defined as a belt of Mexican territory, a few miles wide and one thousand

passable spine-defended *bottoms of the bag*, leaving him to retreat, if he can, with the points of the compass whirling in his head.[2]

While these observations are perhaps expressive of the natural feelings of an observer of a cactus jungle, to the Cisco Kid the demon plant with its blind lures offers no problems; his red roan mount lessens the distance to Tonia Perez's jacal with every step he takes through the countless acres of the prickly *nopal*.

City-bred Chicken Ruggles, the Piggy and Black Eagle of the story in which he appears, steps tremulously along the mat of curly mesquite grass, for he is afraid of snakes, brigands, centipedes, mirages, and fandangoes; but man of the world, Black Bill, takes the rugged landscape "in his stride".[3] To him the country looks like a gentleman's private estate, except that there are no bulldogs to run out and bite at his heels. He observes merely that the grass is shoe-top deep, and that the mesquite trees look like a peach orchard – and that Ogden's ranch shack is about the size of an elevated railroad station.[4]

Along the sloughs and water courses live oak, pecan, and hackberry trees grow thickly. Great expanses of the grassy prairies have been covered over completely by spinous thickets of brush, as impenetrable and forbidding as the bristling pear. These are the *chaparral* or *brasada*, made up mainly of catclaw, mesquite, black brush, and juajilla, all hardy perennials of the Leguminosae family, plants which seem to disdain soil and water and derive their sustenance from the surrounding air.

Besides the Rio Grande, or Bravo del Norte, this great tableland is drained by the rivers Frio and Nueces, and the infinity of waterless creeks, or *arroyos*, draws, and *cañadas* that serve as tributaries to the main streams. It is a peculiarity of the prairie rivers of Texas, noted even by early travellers, that for long distances of their courses they are in reality a succession of pools or holes of water, joined only in the rainy seasons by a continuous

---

miles long, extending from Bagdad at the mouth of the Rio Grande to Chihuahua. Goods were transported duty free in the zone.

2 "The Caballero's Way", *Works*, I, 432.
3 "The Passing of Black Eagle", *Ibid.*, I, 432.
4 "The Hiding of Black Bill", *Ibid.*, I, 699.

surface flow.[5] It was this odd nature of the west Texas streams that prompted a waggish tourist of early days to comment that "the rivers of this region are not navigable – at least not above ground".[6]

Tonio Perez, in "The Caballero's Way", who lives at the edge of the pear, a hundred yards down Arroyo Hondo from Lone Wolf Crossing on the Frio, fills her earthenware jar from a water hole in that stream. Chicken Ruggles finds Bud King's band of stock rustlers at a water hole on the San Miguel;[7] Lieutenant Sandridge camps at a water hole on the Frio while engaged in the delicate business of ensnaring the Cisco Kid.[8] In fact, the water hole before the wind-mill came had a value which a present-day observer can hardly appreciate.

Young Willie Porter came to La Salle county in 1882. He could not have picked a more favorable time – or a better place – to gain acquaintance with material for his desperado stories.

The International & Great Northern, the first railroad to enter the chaparral, had pushed through from San Antonio to Laredo the year before. The newly invented barbed wire had made its appearance some years earlier, and big ranchers and free grass men were in the midst of a great contest over the fencing of the landed domain.[9] Armed bands of fence-cutters played havoc with barbed wire in the three counties between Cotulla and San Antonio. Editorials about fence-cutting depredations filled the papers. In Bexar county there were three bands of cutters, called respectively the *Knights of the Nippers*, the *Order of Javelinas*, the *Blue Devils*. In one night alone five hundred yards of fence were cut within ten miles of San Antonio.[10] The expression, "Keep your fences up", variants of which are encountered often in O. Henry's

[5] N. A. Taylor, *Coming Empire, or Two Thousand Miles in Texas on Horseback*, p. 82. See also "Barbed Wire in Texas", *The Southwestern Historical Quarterly*, LXI, No. 2 (October, 1957).

[6] Alex E. Sweet and J. Armory Knox, *On a Mexican Mustang Through Texas*, XXXVII, 511.

[7] "The Passing of Black Eagle", *Works*, I, 433.

[8] "The Caballero's Way", *ibid.*, I, 202.

[9] San Antonio *Express* (March 2, 1880).

[10] *Ibid.* (February 27, 1884).

Front Street, Cotulla, Texas, about 1884. Courtesy, Mrs. Isabel Gaddis.

stories, was a widely current locution of the time. Barbed wire and the railroad, two of the three factors which were to revolutionize the cattle industry of Texas, had appeared in the chaparral; the third, the windmill, was yet to play its full part.

At this time (1882), Indiana-born Sam Bass, train-robber and hero of cattle-trail and ballad, had met his fate a few years before at Round Rock; Texas' own and greatest "single-handed terror" of all time, John Wesley Hardin, had done five of his seventeen years at Huntsville; King Fisher, riddle of the Rio Grande, now reformed and a deputy sheriff of Uvalde County, had served two peaceful years as an upholder of the law. Ben Thompson as marshal of Austin was, for the time, in a quieter, legal phase of his turbulent career. Chivalrous Ham White, stage and train robber, the Claude Duval of the age, had concluded the Texas chapter of a career that had several more years to run. Ranger Lee "Red" Hall, who had had a hand in checking the lawlessness of all these bandits, had now married, quit the ranger force, and settled down to the more lucrative business of managing the 400,000 acre Dull, Hall and Dull ranch in the Nueces and Frio sectors. Hall had been induced to take up the task of tangling with the fence-cutters because his wife, with many bandits still at large, feared for his safety as a ranger.[11]

Willie Porter came as a visitor to the D. H. & D. ranch, and made his home with Lee's brother Dick, a sheepman, who ran his herds on this immense acreage. Dick's house was not much bigger than an elevated railroad station, and probably looked very much like the shack Black Bill found Henry Ogden occupying.

From Lee Hall and his ex-ranger cowhands young Porter could have learned much of the bandit lore that was to enrich his Texas stories. He could have heard tales of nineteen-year old Lieutenant Wright,[12] fearless and carefree in combat, much like the debonair youth in McNulty's company, who is the envy of Bob Buckley;[13] he could have learned of Philadelphia-born N. A. Jennings, a

[11] An adequate treatment of Hall's stay at the Dull ranch is found in Dora Neil Raymond, *Captain Lee Hall of Texas*, XV, 205.
[12] N. A. Jennings, *A Texas Ranger*, XIV, 113.
[13] "An Afternoon Miracle", *Works*, I, 167.

dead ringer for "the misguided Eastern man, burdened with an education", who speaks of Tybalt and his book of arithmetic; [14] of "Girlie" McKinney, a study for Captain Kinney whom Bud King hides from; [15] and of Captain Leander H. McNelly (O. Henry's McNulty), ranger chieftain who broke up old Juan Cortinas' cattle stealing on the border.

The best known outlaw of the Nueces Strip in those days was J. King Fisher. It was through fear of Fisher mainly that Captain Hall's wife had persuaded the ranger chieftain to leave the service. There is indication in two of O. Henry's stories that the former sojourner at the D. H. & D. ranch was familiar with the whims of the handsome, swashbuckling "enigma of the border". Fisher it was whom tradition says Horace Greeley chided for his reputed wantonness in the use of firearms; Greeley, a report says, met Fisher while on a visit to San Antonio. Of Fisher it is also said that the road leading to his Pendencia ranch had at its entrance this warning sign: "This Is King Fisher's Road. Take the Other." [16] The implication was, of course, that misfortune would betide the thoughtless traveller who failed to exercise the caution the words counseled. Tradition also has it that Fisher once in a capricious mood had his men hold up a circus train just to get him a tiger skin for a pair of chaparreras.

In "The Last of the Troubadours", O. Henry could have had King Fisher in mind when he drew his portrait of King James. King James appears as a vain autocrat of the range, and the biggest cattleman between the Alamo Plaza in Santone and Bill Hopper's saloon in Brownsville. "Also he was the loudest and most offensive bully and braggart and badman in Southwest Texas." (Fisher was said to have kept a record of both those whom he had killed and those whom he intended to kill.)

Sixty-five-year-old, ninety-eight-pound sheepman Sam Ellison is overawed on meeting this formidable two-hundred-pound monarch with sunburned visage and fierce eyes, with sixshooters and millions of cartridges, and a shotgun laid across his saddle.

---

[14]   *Ibid.*, 166.
[15]   "The Passing of Black Eagle", *Works*, I, 433.
[16]   Bruce Roberts, *Springs From the Parched Ground*, p. 66.

O. Henry has sometimes been accused of the American failing of hyperbole; but King James is hardly more of an exaggeration of a living creature than the King Fisher pictured to us by former McNelly ranger, Philadelphia journalist and adventurer, Napoleon Augustus Jennings. Jennings recorded his experiences as a ranger in his book, *A Texas Ranger,* published in 1899. In an account of the capture of Fisher, the Philadelphia journalist thus describes the man:

He was about twenty-five years old at that time, and the most perfect specimen of a frontier dandy and desperado I ever met. He was tall, beautifully, and exceedingly handsome. He wore the finest clothing procurable, but all of the picturesque, border, dime-novel kind. His broad-brimmed white Mexican sombrero was profusely ornamented with gold and silver lace and had a golden snake for a band. His fine buckskin Mexican short jacket was heavily embroidered with gold. His shirt was of the finest and thinnest linen and was worn open at the throat, with a silk handkerchief knotted loosely about the wide collar. A brilliant crimson silk sash was wound about his waist, and his legs were hidden by a wonderful pair of chaparejos, or chaps . . . made of the skin of a royal Bengal tiger. . . . Hanging from his cartridge belt were two ivory-handled, silver plated six-shooters.

O. Henry makes his terrible King James a badman, and the biggest cattleman of his part of the state, a cattle king, in contradistinction to sheepman Sam Ellison, the last of the barons.

Cattle king and badman should not be regarded as an anomalous combination. Elsewhere ("Seats of the Haughty") the author defines the term "cattle king":

In them days, as you know, there was cattle barons and cattle kings. The difference was this: when a cattleman went to Santone and bought beer for the newspaper reporters and only give them the number of cattle he actually owned, they wrote him up for a baron. When he bought 'em champagne wine and added in the amount of the cattle he had stole, they called him a king.

Outlaw King Fisher's method of acquiring "wet" stock from Mexico was hardly less orthodox than the behavior of some of the "kings". Fisher may have reasoned that if Cortinas could rustle cows on this side of the Rio Bravo, it was at least morally within the law for a Texan to cross over and rustle on the other side.

King James (to return to the story), after telling old man Ellison that he has bought the two sections of land on which the man's lease has lately expired, further says to his bewildered victim:

This range you've got your sheep on is mine. I'm putting up a wire fence, forty by sixty miles; and if there's a sheep inside of it when it's done, it'll be a dead one. If they ain't gone by then, I'll send six men over here with Winchesters to make mutton out of the whole lot.[17]

The reader wonders whether these are the words of cattle king or badman, and whether O. Henry had a purpose in portraying King James as having qualities of both. Sheepman Sam Ellison is definitely the victim of the barbed wire entanglements that played havoc with small stockmen in that era. One of the duties of Lee Hall, on taking over the management of the Dull Brothers' holdings, was to acquire the right and title to small tracts joining one another. By April, 1883, Messrs. Dull, Hall and Dull had run their fences round 400,000 acres.[18]

King James embodies all the evil of the syndicate owner and the badman of the stripe of Fisher – although in the story there is no specific point made of the pure desperado aspect of the man – unless it be the demonstration of goodness James makes when he finds that Sam Ellison is kin to the Jackson County Reeves of Mississippi, his native state.

"Now let's re-talk over some things we discussed a few days ago", says the mollified King James when we see him for a second time in conversation with the baron. "They call me a bad man; and they're only half right. There's plenty of room in *my* pasture for your bunch of sheep and their increase for a long time to come."

King James, however, softens too late in his attitude towards Ellison. The old man has made the fateful error of confiding his sad plight to troubadour Sam Galloway,[19] and Galloway, as a

[17]   "The Last of the Troubadours", *Works*, II, 816.
[18]   Dora Neil Raymond, *op. cit.*, XIV, 192.
[19]   Could O. Henry have heard of a real Sam Galloway? This person's

courteous guest, feels obliged to help his host out of his difficulty by "regulating the King's account".

The real desperado, King Fisher, suffered a fate similar to that of King James. After joining the church at a Baptist camp meeting, he had a change of heart and soon became deputy sheriff of Uvalde county.[20] He was such a popular peace officer that it was generally conceded that he would be the next sheriff; but before the election took place, he was murdered in San Antonio while serving as mediator in a difficulty between gamblers Joe Foster and Ben Thompson.

Other traits of the legendary Fisher are represented in the person of Bud King, in "The Passing of Black Eagle". King is here shown, as Fisher was said to be, as an affable man of modest desires who always keeps a sharp lookout for the rangers and is not above exacting stores from supply sources along his ways of travel. King's band is depicted as a funloving, peaceable, unpicturesquely clad group, of gentle manners and soft voices, who could easily be mistaken for a bunch of country bumpkins out for a fish-fry or pecan-gathering. They run off some very good companies of horses from the ranges, drive a few bunches of cattle across the Rio Grande, and dispose of them profitably on the *otro la'o*; and they terrorize Mexican villages and settlements for provisions and ammunition. They escape law officers on both sides of the river without killing any of them (a noteworthy feature in a "western" story), and are content with reasonable profits from their transactions.

When news comes that Captain Kinney (a name suggestive of ranger Captain McKinney) and his men are coming to investigate their actions, the prudent Bud orders the gang to retire for a time to the prickly fastnesses of the Frio bottoms, where they go into camp by a water hole.

The illicit cattle deals, the horse transactions, the terrorizing of the villages and settlements for food and provender, and retire-

---

death had been reported in the *Express*. "Sam Galloway died at Columbus, Ohio, a few weeks ago. His force was in his face-makings. He could make a first rate speech without uttering a syllable." San Antonio *Express* (April 26, 1872).

[20]   Bruce Roberts, *op. cit.*, p. 68.

ment to a place of hiding when the rangers are in "hot pursuit" are all echoes of routine incidents in the career of Fisher. And the thumbnail sketch of the genial Bud, idol of his peaceable, fun-loving companions, is in tenor not unlike accounts left us of the resourceful border chieftain.

N. A. Jennings records an incident that illustrates Fisher's affability. Once while on a scout for desperadoes, says Jennings, he and ranger Bill McKinney went into a saloon in Eagle Pass. They had not been in the place long before the noted King Fisher himself walked in.

"Whoopee!" cried the king. "All the rangers have gone down the river. Everybody come up to the bar and have a drink!"

McKinney and Jennings walked up and placed themselves on each side of Fisher.

"Well, gosh durn my chaps", said the outlaw, recognizing them. "I thought you boys were all down the river. ... Do you want me for anything?"

When told that they did, Fisher handed over his white-handled six-shooters, and after drinking with the rangers, went to their camp, and that night accompanied some of them to a fandango.

Fisher on this occasion, as usual, gave bail and was released.[21]

While Lee Hall was in Austin in January, 1877, making plans to take over the command of the ailing ranger chieftain, Leander H. McNelly, he was ordered to hurry from the city to the scene of a daylight stage robbery that had taken place on the Camino Real between Austin and San Antonio.[22] When Hall, after a chase, caught the robbers in Luling they proved to be one Ham White and a young man whom White in a thoughtless moment had employed in the only recorded instance of his detaining a stage-coach with a helper.

On confessing, White established himself as the highwayman who had been looting stages in and out of Austin for several years. For color, daring, and gallantry, White has been likened to Claude Duval, notorious English knight of the road, whose death was the subject of a satiric ode by Samuel Butler.

---

[21] N. A. Jennings, *op. cit.*, XVII, 133.
[22] San Antonio *Express* (March 30, 1877).

White was a robber with a definite code of ethics. Unlike Duval, who was modest in his demands of his female victims, the Texas highwayman refrained from molesting women altogether. As far as his observation would enable him to estimate the status of his victims, he took from them only according to their ability to pay.

Except in the one careless instance that proved his undoing, he worked alone. He would sit his horse while a robbery was in progress, urging passengers or coachman, with a wave of his pistol, to hand over their valuables or rip open the mail bags. When a driver once protested the command to slash a mail pouch, saying he had taken an oath to protect the U. S. mails, White patted his revolver, and declared: "This is the oath you're to obey." He was considerate enough, however, to make those who rifled the sacks at his bidding keep the contents of each separate, avowing that he did not want to put the Government to any unnecessary inconvenience.

Many are the stories told of White's warped notions of generosity. Once one of his victims was a young man from Tennessee, from whom White took a thousand dollars that the man declared he had been saving for years to go into the grocery business. On hearing the tale, the bandit hastily returned $200, and promised to send more later, saying that industry deserved a reward. On an occasion when White relieved a clergyman of his watch, that gentleman asked the highwayman if he would rob a minister of the gospel of a cherished gift.

"I don't know", White is reported to have answered, as he hesitated. "What church do you belong to?"

The minister stated his church.

White emitted a befitting oath, and said: "Here. Take your watch back. I belong to that church myself."

During the robbery that led to his capture, White at the outset had taken $54 and a watch from Corbin, the stage driver. After picking up $900 from the passengers and $500 in a registered letter, he returned Corbin his watch, explaining that since he had done so well, "You can have your watch back."

White was tried and sentenced to 99 years in the Moundsville,

W. Va., penitentiary for robbing the U. S. mails. A near relative of Secretary of the Navy Goff, he was pardoned by President Hayes – the granting of the pardon being the last act of Hayes' official life.[23]

Later White robbed stages and trains in Colorado under the name of Burton.[24] He was again caught and sentenced to life imprisonment, but escaped, and when last heard of was robbing stages in California, always alone and often identified with Black Bart,[25] a notorious highwayman of the period.

Mr. Ham White is thus depicted as a ubiquitous road-agent of rare intelligence and valuable connections, of solitary habits and quaint humor, with an uncanny knack for working himself out of ticklish situations.

O. Henry's Ham, called Black Bill, in "The Hiding of Black Bill", has habits and manners that suggest a close kinship with Ham White.

As the "strong, red-faced man with a Wellington beak and small, fiery eyes tempered by flaxen lashes" sits on the railroad station platform at Los Piños, he is thus addressed by his fat, seedy companion:

"Ain't seen you in about four years, Ham. Which way you been travelling?"

Ham then tells of his flight to the thorny fastnesses of the Nueces country in Texas after robbing an M. K. & T. train, revealing at the end of his account that he is Black Bill.

The Ham of the story "hides out" under the very appropriate brush country name of Percival St. Clair, on the sheep ranch of a

---

[23] In the Houston *Post* (March 30, 1881), we read: "Ham White, convicted in U. S. court at Austin about four years ago for stage robbery and sentenced for life to U. S. pen at Moundsville, W. Va., arrived at his home near Bastrop, last Saturday, having been pardoned by the president. The petition for his pardon was signed by almost every man in the county."

[24] N. A. Jennings, *op. cit.*, XIX, 148.

[25] Black Bart, the "Po. 8", as he called himself, landed in the state penitentiary at San Quentin, December 4, 1883. Black Bart, single-handed, was said "to have committed more robberies than perhaps any other solitary individual in the annals of crime, for he robbed the stages of the Wells-Fargo Express on the Pacific coast twenty-eight times within a few years". San Antonio *Express* (December 10, 1883).

man named Henry Ogden. Ham takes the job of tending Ogden's flocks, but soon the wool enters his soul and Nature gets next to him. Ogden one evening, trying to mitigate the loneliness of his herder, brings out a deck of cards, and the two play casino, stimulating their spirits by partaking occasionally from a decanter of bourbon which the rancher has fetched from a cupboard.

"Do you remember reading in the papers about a month ago," says Ogden, "about a train hold-up on the M. K. & T.? The express agent was shot through the shoulder and about $15,000 in currency taken. And it is said that only one man did the job."

"Was there any description mentioned of this single-handed terror?" asks Ham.

"Why, no," says Ogden; "because they say nobody got a good sight of him because he wore a mask. But they know it was a train robber called Black Bill, because he always works alone, and because he dropped a handkerchief in the express car that had his name on it."[26]

The two then engage in a quantity of non-committal conversation that leaves the reader wondering if Ogden is not Black Bill.

Ham, or Black Bill, has also a facetious vein that marks him as a robber of the same order as Ham White and Black Bart. To quote the character again:

Mr. Ogden, you and me have got to get sociable. Sheep are all very well to dot the landscape and furnish eight-dollar cotton suitings for man, but for table talk and fireside companions they rank along with five o'clock teazers. If you've got a deck of cards, or a parcheesi outfit, or a game of authors, get 'em out, and let's get on a mental basis. I've got to do something in an intellectual line, if it's only to knock somebody's brains out.[27]

Ham White, in a less ingenious way, would also express his humor: "Don't you know it's wicked to rob the U. S. mail?" he teased a victim who slit open the mail sacks at the point of his

---

[26] "On the third of November the stage was robbed on the Sonora route, and nearly $5000 obtained by the *lone highwayman*, who, being shot was compelled to hurry, and in the excitement of the chase dropped a handkerchief and cuff, which in the subsequent search were found by Sheriff Thorn.... They having Chinese laundry marks, led to his early arrest here...". *Ibid.*

[27] "The Hiding of Black Bill", *Works*, I, 700.

revolver. "I'd make a complaint against you if I had time to fool around the courts as a witness." [28]

The fictional Ham possesses, too, in common with the real Ham (and surprisingly for a practicing outlaw of either fact or fancy), the very natural trait of fear.

Five armed men have ridden up to the ranch house, and confronting Black Bill, the boss "swings his gun over till the opening in it seems to cover [Bill's] whole front elevation." The boss states his reason for coming and then asks Black Bill his name.

"Captain", says the flustered Black Bill, "Percival St. Clair is my occupation, and my name is sheep-herder. I've got my flock of veals – no muttons – penned here to-night. The searchers are coming to-morrow to give them a haircut . . ."

Captain Lee Hall and his three ranger companions surrounded White as he hurriedly and uneasily tightened the cinches of his saddle in a passage-way of a Luling livery stable. Hall walked up closer to the nervous man and addressed him casually.

"Don't come near me," warned White.

"Why, you look scared," said Hall.

"It's enough to scare anybody to be surrounded by three or four men," the highwayman replied.

Hall and his men then closed in on White pretty much as the posse does on Ogden when they throw him down and take the tell-tale Espinosa City Bank bills from his pocket. Hall found $4000 and incriminating memoranda in White's pockets. [29]

Detective Ben Price, who refuses to recognize heroic Jimmy Valentine (alias Ralph D. Spencer) in "A Retrieved Reformation", and leaves the former safe-cracker free, presumably to enjoy his new-found happiness, behaves somewhat in the same manner as did detective John Price of the Texas Detective Agency of San Antonio. John Price one day received an order to "arrest and hold" Marshall Tate Polk, the $400,000 defaulting treasurer of the state of Tennessee. The absconding Tennessee official had arrived in the Alamo City on the G. H. & S. A. train from New

[28]   N. A. Jennings, *op. cit.*, XIX, 147.
[29]   Dora Neil Raymond, *op. cit.*, II, 84.

Orleans and made his way across town to the I. & G. N. depot, apparently with the intention of fleeing to Mexico. Polk had two valises fully packed, one with greenbacks and another with gold specie. The suitcase full of gold, one may presume, was every bit as heavy as Ralph Spencer's case of burgular instruments. After holding Polk all day, Price let him go, claiming he could not identify his man.[30]

Two days later, U. S. Marshal Hal Gosling brought Polk back from Laredo to San Antonio; and two months later the marshal received a reward of $9730 for the capture of Polk.[31]

The Galveston *News* (January 20, 1883) carried a story taken from the Louisville *Courier Journal* that tells a fact or two about the unsavory record of Price. Once in New Orleans Price had effected the release of a noted bank-robber, one Forrester, in the hopes of receiving some of the thief's booty. Still later, Captain Lee Hall of the Texas Rangers had felt the need of beating Price over the head with his own revolver. The *News* writer concluded his article by saying that "police authorities and noted detectives of this city" are certain that "Detective Price" must have secured a large sum of money from Mr. Treasurer Polk.

Thus in both instances, the real and the fancied, heavy suitcases are involved, and a detective by the name of Price feels that he has no reason to detain his man.

This incident of the counterfeit sleuth and the over-weight luggage should not be dismissed without incorporating here a passage from the story in which Jimmy Valentine appears.[32] Annabel Adams, the banker's daughter, whom Valentine, as Ralph D. Spencer, is shortly to marry, is in a joyous mood as her betrothed makes ready to leave for Little Rock to buy his wedding clothes. She puts on his hat and picks up the suitcase filled with the burglar's tools.

"My! Ralph, how heavy it is. Feels like it was full of gold bricks."

"Lot of nickel-plated shoe-horns in there," says Jimmy, coolly,

---

[30] San Antonio *Express* and Houston *Post* (January 9, 1883).
[31] See the story of Dick Price in Al Jennings, *Through the Shadows with O. Henry*, XVIII, XIX.
[32] "A Retrieved Reformation", *Works*, I, 438.

"that I'm going to return. Thought I'd save express charges by taking them up. I'm getting awfully economical."

The next segment of this discussion could very aptly bear the title, "Mr. William S. Porter Adapts a Train Robbery". The alleged adaptation is embodied in – in fact, is the central part of – the narrative of the strange dream of Shark Dodson, Wall Sreet broker.[33]

On November 26, 1883, the San Antonio *Express* reported that the east-bound Southern Pacific Express train had been robbed near the little town of Flatonia, Texas. Three masked men took part in the hold-up, and although the take was said to be light, somewhat under $1000, engineer T. C. Webster was killed when he attempted to defend himself. The robbers then held up the express messenger and went through the express mail. John Price, alias Johnny Over-the-Fence, was thought to be leader of the gang.

This was one of the first robberies in the history of the Southern Pacific railroad. Less than a year before Thomas Wentworth Peirce's Sunset railroad, heading west, had joined Collis P. Huntington's Southern Pacific, east-bound. A ceremony commemorating the union of the two lines had taken place on January 12, 1882, near the Pecos river.

Shark Dodson, Bob Tidball and John Big Dog, the three chevaliers of industry in "The Roads We Take", are more successful in their haul when they stop the Sunset Express twenty miles from Tucson. The $30,000 they pick up from the express car is divided equally between Dodson, the leader, and Tidball, when the express messenger terminates John Big Dog's earthly career with a shot from his Winchester. Leader Dodson shortly thereafter is forced to end Tidball's career when the latter's horse pulls up lame. The business of killing Tidball is a matter of expediency with Dodson, whose mount, Bolivar, cannot carry double.

When "Captain Dick", or Brack Cornett was shot and killed at Pearsall, Texas, on February 13, 1888 (the San Antonio *Express*

---

[33] "The Roads We Take", *Works*, II, 1174.

reported), he was declared to have "led a gang of men who boarded a Southern Pacific train at Flatonia, on June 18, 1887, compelled the engineer to run the train about a mile and a half east of town and there stop, when he proceeded to go through the cars and rob the passengers of money and valuables".

This same journal of Jan. 31, 1888, carried an item to the effect that Ed Reeves, last of the McNeil and Flatonia train robber gang, had been captured. Two of his partners, Tom Jones and Bill Humphry, previously captured, were then in jail awaiting trial.

It can be deduced rather readily from these bits of news that by 1888 train robberies were becoming a sort of routine business with the Southern Pacific railroad company; and that these hold-ups were perpetrated usually by a group of three men, with said groups electing as their field of operations the vicinity or environs of the city of Flatonia. It is little wonder that Wall Street broker Shark Dodson would chose two pals to help him rob the Southern Pacific Express (since the custom of robbing in threes had become so well established); nor, because of the nature of Shark's occupation, are we surprised to see him raise the take to $30,000. The wonder is that he would designate Tucson instead of Flatonia as his sphere of action.

There is much in the method Calliope Catesby uses for relief when affected with the megrims that leads one to believe that this hypochondriac of the musical pistols owes his genesis to Ben Thompson, the impetuous, unpredictable, and uncurbed city marshal and gambler of Austin. O. Henry's creation is a more genteel chap than Ben, his ostensible means of livelihood more respectable, his method of warning the citizenry of his armed sallies a bit more primitive, but he has enough in common with "Roaring Ben" to be accounted a close relation.

Buck Walton, friend and legal counsel of Thompson, (the peace-officer's Boswell, in fact), in his life of the gunman, published in the year of the latter's tragic death with King Fisher in San Antonio, pictures his subject as a loving husband and father, with a deep devotion to his old mother – as long as Ben remained sober.[34] When animated by strong spirits, Ben behaved so un-accountably that when again normal he would sometimes apolo-gize to the persons he had offended – if those persons were still alive. Often, when "liquored up", he would be seized with the urge of repentance and reform.

Walton relates that once when feeling that he was corrupting the youth of Austin, Ben shot up his own gambling parlor.[35] This untoward act was performed greatly to the consternation of his "pardner", one Loraine, who was in despair on seeing bullets from Ben's six-shooters perforating the keno goose, roulette wheels, and faro tables. Prompted by this same urge of reform, Ben, one Christmas night, raided the Senate Bar and Variety Theatre, both run by the notorious Wilson, and ended his spree by killing that genial proprietor.[36] It was a coincidence, of course, that Wilson's place of business was drawing a large number of Ben's former patrons.

Still keenly sensitive to the problem of social reform, later, while city marshal of Austin, Ben journeyed to San Antonio and killed his old acquaintance, Jack Harris, one-armed ex-scout of Sidney Johnston's in the Mormon War. After losing heavily at Jack's faro table, Ben suddenly realized that the game was crooked. He openly made such a charge and declared that the joint was a trap of iniquity corrupting the morals of the young men of San Antonio. Harris resented the imputation. An armed *rencontre* followed the next day. Before Harris could wheel his shotgun into action, a bullet from Ben's pistol had laid him low.[37]

Thompson was kept in jail for six months pending trial for this killing, much to the anger and disgust of the Austin citizenry. It was a relief to these people when the man was finally tried and acquitted. On his return to Austin with his wife and children he was met at the train by a host of admirers; they welcomed him with speeches, presented him with flowers, and, removing the

---

[34] Wm. W. Walton, *Life and Adventures of Ben Thompson, the Famous Texan,* p. 190.

[35] *Ibid.,* p. 147.

[36] *Ibid.,* p. 159.

[37] San Antonio *Express* (July 12, 1882). (The contention between these two opposites is treated more fully elsewhere in this work.)

Congress Avenue, Austin, about 1884
(I. and G.N.R.R. Depot in Background).

horses from the carriage he had entered, pulled the hero up Congress Avenue themselves, a brass band playing a triumphal march as the celebrants travelled along.[38]

A notable instance of Ben's "shooting up the town", in Calliope Catesby fashion, occurred after the gunman's defeat in his first attempt at election to the office of town marshal. Downcast at the rejection of his offer of leadership, Thompson, after ample warning of his intentions, buckled on his armor and went forth to play havoc up the Avenue. He shot up the Iron Front saloon (an institution he had sold a few weeks before); took a few pot shots at a former rival drinking establishment; sent a few bullets whizzing into the office of the Austin *Statesman* (an error in judgment, for the *Statesman* was a friendly newspaper); blasted the insides out of an organ-grinder's instrument; sent a few spite tokens into police headquarters; and, his fit of sorrow still upon him, fled from the scene of his chagrin on the M. K. & T. Katy Flier – and was not seen again in Austin for two years. When he came back, he again sought the office of marshal, and this time the electorate yielded.[39]

Thompson's career as a peace-officer (as we have seen) ended in his bloody murder with King Fisher at Jack Harris's old variety theatre in San Antonio on March 11, 1884. O. Henry arrived in Austin the day after Ben's funeral, and could have read in the *Daily Dispatch* of the "vast concourse of people" who saw the martyr's body consigned to its final resting place.

Calliope Catesby is O. Henry's study of the Thompson style of frontier eccentric. The splenetic Calliope, terror of the village of Quicksand, a place not unlike early Cotulla, announces the start of one of his sorties by the fearful, brassy yell that has caused the townspeople to tack onto him the name of the steam piano. Then he unlimbers his guns to test his aim.

A yellow dog, the personal property of Colonel Swazey, proprietor of the Occidental Hotel, falls feet upward in the dust with one farewell yelp. The new gilt weather-cock on Judge Riley's lemon and ultramarine two-story residence shivers, flaps, and hangs by a splinter.

38 Wm. W. Walton, *op. cit.*, p. 189.
39 *Ibid.*, p. 173.

... Down the street goes Calliope, shooting right and left. Glass falls like hail; dogs vamose; chickens fly, squawking; feminine voices shriek concernedly to youngsters at large. The din is perforated at intervals by the staccato of the Terror's guns.[40]

Buck Patterson and two deputies, less mindful of Catesby's warning than the Austin police were of Ben's admonitory notice, set about at once in making an effort to "gather in the Terror". Their first volley breaks the lock on one of Catesby's guns, explodes a cartridge in his cross belt, and cuts a neat underbit in his right ear. Thompson, according to Walton, once by design "marked" a San Saba rowdy by drilling a neat hole in his right ear. And just as Ben had finally ended his foray at the railroad station, so does Catesby end his. The Terror gives a final demonstration of his pistol wizardry by barkin' Bud Patterson just as the train arrives. On the train comes Catesby's old mother, who, knowing nothing of her son's perverse behavior, puts the son in an embarrassing situation when she greets him. He saves face by pinning the unconscious marshal's badge on his chest to deceive his unsuspecting mother. On regaining his senses and seeing Catesby's predicament, Patterson joins in the deception and helps keep up the fiction as long as the old lady stays in Quicksand.

There are other particulars, too, in this story of the roarer, the badman who "treed" the town, that show kinship with instances in the career of the incorrigible Ben. Both Catesby and Thompson profess a deep, perhaps maudlin, attachment to their mothers; Catesby is forty-one years old – his mother tells this to Patterson in the touching scene at the railroad station – the very age of Thompson when he died.[41] Catesby, as Thompson often did, shows a kind of remorse; and likewise, as did his prototype in the flesh, attains the marshal's badge.

The "roarer", or town hell-raiser, had long before attracted the attention of another and earlier Southwestern master of humorous satire, George Washington Harris. In one of his Sut Lovingood yarns, "Contempt of Court – Almost", Harris makes his star performer, Sut, give a sympathetic account of how Wirt Staples

---

[40]   "The Reformation of Calliope", *Works*, I, 261.
[41]   Wm. W. Walton, *op. cit.*, p. 194.

"got" Jedge Smarty and "help't tu 'stonish ole Doltin'", the sheriff. Staples is a creature of a wild and extravangant fancy, not altogether unlike Rabelais' conception of Pantagruel, who uses Loupgarou as a scythe in his contest with the giants.[42] Staples has changed his doggery, and the three horns of the spirits he has drunk in the new liquor-house hoists his tail and sets his bristles "bout as stiff es eight of the uther doggery juice wud". About nine in the morning, when court convened, Wirt was "well-oiled" and ready for a sortie abroad. Sut Lovingood, himself, now takes up the story:

"The hollerin stage ove the disease now struck him, so he roa'd one good year-quiverin roar, an' riz three foot inside the doggery door, an' lit nine more out in the mud, sploshin hit all over the winders, tuther side of the street. He had a dried venerson ham in one han, an' a ten-year old nigger by hits gallus-crossin in tuther. He waved fus' the nigger an' then the venerson over his head, steppin short an' high, like ontu a bline hoss, an' lookin squar atwixt his shoe-heels, wif his shoulders hump'd hi up. Sez he,
    " 'Hu – wee,' clear an' loud es a tin ho'n, 'run onder the hen, yere's the blue-tail hawk, an' he's a-flyin' low. . . . Then he roared a time ur two, an' look'd up an' down the street, like a bull looks fur tuther one, when he thinks he hearn him beller. He riz ontu his tip-toes, an' finished a good loud 'Hu – wee.' "

The cry of "Hu-wee" would sound like the music of a calliope only if it were uttered with the proper intonation. The venison ham and the little nigger just remotely resemble the two six-guns of Catesby; but no one would say that the two objects do not contribute to the two-gun effect. Certainly Staples is able to do considerable damage with his armament. Witness the havoc he causes with the little "imp of midnite":

"He flung hit up'ards, an' es hit cum down, hit met one ove Wirt's boots. Away his flew, spread like ontu a flyin squirrel, smash thru a watch-tinker's winder, totin in broken sash, an' glass, an' bull's-eye watches, an' sasser watches, an' spoons, an' doll heads, an' clay pipes, an' fishin reels, an' sum noise. A ole ball-headed cuss wer a-sittin a-peepin intu a ole watch, arter spiders, wif a thing like a big black wart kiverin one eye, when the smashery cum, an' the fus' thing he

[42] François Rabelais, *Gargantua and Pantagruel*, I, 233.

knowed, he wer flat ove his back, wif a small, pow'fully skeer'd ash-
culler'd nigger, a struddil his naik, littil bras wheels spinnin on the
floor, an' watches singin like rattil snakes all roun." [43]

So much for Wirt Staples, an early example of the roaring type
of gentleman, and a worthy ancestor of Calliope Catesby, who
makes himself so offensive to the peace and dignity of the city
of Quicksand.

No other desperado of this tragic era gained a wider reputation
as a gunman than the Texas-born author, inventor, one-man-
army, and school teacher, John Wesley Hardin. The son of a
Methodist preacher and circuit rider, Hardin was in his teens
during the carpetbag and scalawag regime, and like many other
of his wayward contemporaries may be spoken of as a product
of the Reconstruction. The boy was a fiery-tempered individualist,
with a somewhat inflated sense of honor and a remarkable ability
in the use of firearms.

Ranger Napoleon Augustus Jennings records that Hardin could
take a six-shooter in each hand and put twelve bullets in a playing-
card with lightning speed at twenty yards.[44] Texas trail-drivers
avow that at eighteen Wess made Wild Bill Hickok put up his guns
when marshal of Abilene, Kansas.[45] Wess devised the "road-
agent's spin" and invented the shoulder-holster. No man could
handle his guns with greater ease than he.

By the time he was seventeen he had killed ten men (mostly
carpetbag Governor E. J. Davis's state police), and, as a result,
was "on the dodge". Hidden, befriended, often cornered, and
showered with gifts of money by citizens who feared the Negro
state police, as rewards for his capture grew Wess headed for
Mexico, went up the trail to Kansas instead, and returned on the
run with dead Indians, a Mexican murderer, and a few gamblers
and thieves making a bloody wake along his path.

There was nothing mean or little about Wess Hardin. He never

[43]   George W. Harris, "Contempt of Court – Almost", *Sut Lovingood*, 244-
255.
[44]   N. A. Jennings, *op. cit.*, XIX, 150.
[45]   Charles A. Siringo, *Riata and Spurs*, p. 138.

stole a horse or cow, or robbed a train, or shot up a town, and wanted only reasonable pay for his expenses the time he chased down and killed the blood-thirsty Bideño. He did play cards, and bet on race-horses (of which animals he owned a few fast ones himself), and traded a good deal in horses and cattle – in a more or less lawful way. He felt that all his killings were justified – every man he killed was trying to kill him – or at least he had a mind to, which in Wess's judgment was the same thing.

Hardin was so handsome, youthful, and innocent looking that friend and foe alike doubted the tales of his villainy. When at twenty-one Wess rubbed out his fortieth victim and an angry mob hanged his brother Joe and cousins Bud and Tom Dixon (perhaps only to show their spite), the outlaw found it expedient to remove to Florida. Four years later he was captured in that state by rangers and brought back to Texas to serve sixteen years for the murder of his last victim.

The Hardin of both fact and legend is sometimes seriously, sometimes playfully, presented "as killing men on slight provocation, and on no provocation at all. He never forgave an injury, and to incur his displeasure was simply suicide." [46]

The Cisco Kid of "The Caballero's Way" is an example of the Hardin type of desperado.[47]

He killed for the love of it – because he was quicktempered – to avoid arrest – for his own amusement – any reason that came to his mind would suffice.
The ... Kid had killed six men in more or less fair scrimmages, had murdered twice as many ..., and had winged a larger number whom he modestly forebore to count. Therefore a woman loved him.[48]

Hardin calmly tells of his marriage to Jane Bowen shortly after he had killed three of a posse who had come from Austin to arrest him:

Nothing of importance happened until I married Jane Bowen, though we were expecting the police to come any time. They would have

[46]   N. A. Jennings, *op. cit.*, XIX, 150.
[47]   Texas newspapers of the 70's and 80's carried frequent notices of robberies committed by members of a band known as the Cisco Roughs.
[48]   "The Caballero's Way", *Works*, I, 202.

met with a warm reception in those times, when the marriage bells
were ringing around.[49]

We may wonder whether it was the youthful attractiveness of
Hardin – who was of the age given for the Kid – or his "bravery"
in the face of trouble that engendered love in his sweetheart.

The Cisco Kid, like Hardin, was a ticklish subject of conversation among his acquaintances – and even among his friends.
When ranger Lieutenant Sandridge made inquiries of the Kid
among the Mexicans, they all vehemently denied any knowledge
of him. If it had been the Kid's pastime to kill members of their
kind just to see them kick, what would be the penalties he would
exact if they angered him, they reasoned.

Storekeeper Fink observes to Sandridge:

No use to ask them Mexicans. They're afraid to tell. This hombre
they call the Kid's been in my store once or twice. I've an idea you
might run across him – but I guess I don't care to say myself. I'm
two seconds later in pulling a gun than I used to be and the difference
is worth thinking about.[50]

One day in the town of Cuero, Wess Hardin is reputed to have
bet a friend that he could kill with one shot a stranger sitting on
a drygoods box two blocks away. The bet was accepted. Hardin
fired away, and won his bet, and then serenely walked back into
the saloon to take the drink he had coming to him.[51]

Citizens of Cuero were as reluctant as the Mexicans in the
story to admit any knowledge of the fearful badman.

"Were they all afraid of him, and had he no friends?" queried a
visitor to Cuero not long after Hardin's days.

"Well, not many friends," the citizen replied. "He had some admirers; but they did not care to say anything, even in his favor, because Wess was too careless. He would hear that a man had been
talking about him; and then, without asking what the man had said
would fill him full of lead, and afterward ask what lies the scoundrel
had been telling about him." [52]

[49]   *The Life of John Wesley Hardin, As Written by Himself*, p. 64.
[50]   "The Caballero's Way", *Works*, I, 203.
[51]   N. A. Jennings, *op. cit.*, XIX, 151.
[52]   Sweet and Knox, *op. cit.*, p. 270.

In his autobiography (published the year after his death in 1895) Hardin indicates that it was a favorite practice of his to outwit his captors or would-be captors and escape, almost always after having taken revenge. In one notable instance he disguised himself as a wounded Confederate veteran to put an "uppety" freedman in his place – a task he accomplished, miraculously without finding the need to shed blood. Once, too, when discovered in the presence of a girl by a man who claimed to be her lover, Hardin played the innocent frightened youth he looked like, lured his tormentor out into a stable, and then, to the surprise and chagrin of the fellow, let him have a full dose of lead.[53]

O. Henry successfully combines the disguise and revenge motifs in his story. When the Kid overhears his love, Tonia, plot with ranger Sandridge to entrap him before his visit is over, he could easily flee at that point, but being a man, like Hardin, who cannot overlook an injury, he plans revenge. An adherent of a code that forbids him from personally harming a woman who has done him wrong, the Kid hatches a scheme that satisfies all his requirements. He intercepts the letter Tonia has written to Sandridge and substitutes one of his own, which he pretends has come from her.

"Dear One," he begins. "To escape he says he will dress in my clothes, my red skirt and the blue waist I wear and the brown mantilla over the head and thus ride away. But before that he says that I must put on his clothes, his *pantalones* and *camisa* and hat and ride away on his horse from the *jacal*. . . ." [54]

The Kid sees that the letter reaches the hands of Sandridge and the ranger falls into the trap. The Kid does precisely the opposite of what he says in the letter he will do: he rides away in his own clothes, and the ranger captain, satisfied with the information he has received, pumps five bullets into the escaping figure in female attire – his newly acquired love, Tonia Perez. The Kid rides away unscathed, exulting in his revenge.

This story should not be dismissed without noting another question it poses: could any of the desperadoes practicing their profession in Texas in that era write such a clear, well-ordered

53   John Wesley Hardin, *op. cit.*, p. 24.
54   "The Caballero's Way", *Works*, I, 209.

letter as the Cisco Kid is represented as doing? Certainly school
teacher, author, lawyer John Wesley Hardin could easily put his
thoughts on paper. Subjoined are a few lines from a letter he
wrote his wife about her brother, Brown Bowen, who was about
to hang for the murder which the unfortunate creature attributed
to John Wesley:

"Jane, dearest, I think as much of your pa and family as ever and
blame him for nothing, although I have been badly treated. Dear
one, on your account and sister Matt's I forgive your pa. He and
Matt send their love to you and family. Dear one, your pa wanted
to know if there was a statement I could make that would save
Brown. I told him no, not an honorable, truthful one. . . ." [55]

Hardin, too, had the Kid's fondness for the "Dear one" formula.

"A Chaparral Christmas Gift", another story on the revenge
theme, could have been inspired by two unusual incidents in the
Sutton-Taylor feud. After Jim Taylor, chief of his faction in this
most famous of all Texas feuds, had shot and killed rival feudist
Bill Sutton, exclaiming as he fired, "Here's something for you!"
he tought it wise to hide while the flurry stirred up by this aggres-
sive act died down. Nearly a year later, as the Christmas season ap-
proached, Jim evidently concluded that the killing was an old enough
event to warrant his moving about again with a fair amount of
safety. He and two of his followers, one Hendricks and Winchester
Smith, chose the festive season to make a call on one of their
friends who lived in a secure, out-of-the way region in the country.
But Jim and his friends had hardly had time to enter into the
celebration planned by their host when word was brought to them
that some of the Sutton boys were outside with a "surprise" for
Jim Taylor. Jim, possibly out of consideration for his host, hastily
fled from the house with his two friends into the darkness of the
surrounding woodland. None of the three, however, was lucky
enough to escape as O. Henry's Madison Lane does with only an
underbit in the right ear. One after another they fell, riddled with
bullets, as they tried to cross a cotton field. [56]

This case of the deadly exchange of leaden greetings had come

[55]   John Wesley Hardin, *op. cit.*, p. 138.
[56]   C. Douglas, *Famous Texas Feuds*, p. 80.

to the attention of Lee Hall when sent to Cuero with ranger leader Leander NcNelly. Later, as Captain Hall, he participated in the most unusual occurrence of his eventful career. With seventeen men he raided the home of the bride's father while a wedding party was in progress. It had developed that the bridegroom and six of the guests and next of kin had been indicted for murder. Naturally, the newly married couple were pretty much upset at the rude interruption of the conjugal festivities. The husband, whose name was Joe Sitterlee, vowed he would resist the "unwarranted" intrusion of the law. But when Hall ordered him to send the women out of the house and prepare for battle, Sitterlee weakened; soon all the men in the party had stacked arms. Then the bride herself appeared to make a request.

After all, she said, a girl's marriage did count for something ... and wouldn't the lieutenant be kind enough to let the party run its course? Lee Hall laughed and gave his sanction. The band struck up and the dance went on – as merrily as though nothing had occurred.[57]

The idea of lead pellets for gifts – one of them a Christmas token – and the notion of the interrupted wedding celebration, are neatly fused in "A Chaparral Christmas Gift". In this story Johnny McRoy, rankled by his failure to win Rosita, descends upon the McMullen-Lane wedding feast when it is at its liveliest, and "yells shrilly at the door, with his forty-five in his hand": "I'll give you a Christmas present!"

His first shot cuts a neat underbit in Mad Lane's right ear, and his second doubtless would have laid the bride low had not Carson, a sheepman, thrown a plate of venison and frijoles to spoil McRoy's aim. This jealousy-bitten lover, unlike the Cisco Kid, is no respecter of codes. Nor does McRoy, like the Suttons at the Taylor Christmas doings, wait outside for his man – perhaps because the intended victim is the host – and the latter, too, escapes vengeance with only the underbit in his ear. Carson, however, recovering his gun from where the guests had hung their arms, does fall from a McRoy bullet as he pursues the avenger into the darkness.

---

[57] *Ibid.*, p. 91.

The cattlemen immediately gather their pistols, sweep out of the house and drive McRoy away. He frolics about for three years with unrestrained lawlessness as the Frio Kid; then he recalls, as another Yule season approaches, the present he had failed to deliver to Mad Lane. He adroitly contrives to be the Santa Claus at the Lane's Christmas doings, devised mainly for the entertainment of the Lane's three-year-old son. In his Santa's garb, McRoy overhears Rosita declare she doesn't think he is wholly bad.

"There's a spot of good somewhere in everybody," she says.
"I heard what you said through the window, Mrs. Lane," says the Frio Kid. "I was just going down in my pocket for a Christmas present for your husband. But I've left one for you instead. It's in the room to the right."

Of course the Kid means Mad Lane. And after this act of goodness, McRoy suffers a disgraceful death at the hands of a bewildered Mexican sheepherder, who hardly knows what he is about when he fires his *pistola*.

Another story of O. Henry's that embodies a clever adaptation of a dramatic incident of the border sagas is "Jimmy Hayes and Muriel". Hayes, a droll humorist with his pet horned toad, is sent by Captain McLean to join a ranger troop on the eve of a hot engagement with a band of Mexican desperadoes under Sebastiano Saldar. In a running fight, the Mexicans escape across the Rio Grande; leaving the ranger force intact, except for Jimmy Hayes, who cannot be found. The young fellow's disappearance is so mysterious and complete that all of the troop are led to believe that he whose bravery under fire was unknown to them, has fled as a coward from his first engagement. A year later, however, the rangers discover what has really happened to their untried comrade. In a big hog-wallow they find the skeletons of three Mexicans whose decomposed bodies can be recognized only by remnants of their attire. "The largest of the figures had once been Sebastiano Saldar. His great, costly sombrero, heavy with gold ornamentation – a hat famous along the border – lay there pierced by three bullets."

Fifty yards away, in another depression, lies another body in common ranchman's clothes, with his rifle bearing upon the three.

The rangers think the body is that of some cowboy, caught alone, who gave a good account of himself – they think this until "from underneath the weatherbeaten rags of the dead man" there crawls a horned toad. The ranger troop now know: there had been a contest of extermination between the recruit-comrade and the Mexican bravos. The members of the troop herd close, and a strange requiem follows. They give a wild yell "which is at once a dirge, an apology, and an epitaph, and a paean of triumph".

There are elements in Captain McNelly's Laguna Madre fight that suggest the Hayes-Saldar combat. In the Laguna Madre affair McNelly and his company of seventeen troopers wiped out a gang of fifteen Mexican cattle thieves, all bravos of the famous Juan Nepomuceno Cortinas. McNelly himself killed the *jefe* or chieftain, Guadalupe Espiñosa.

Napoleon A. Jennings, who was with McNelly, gives an account of the engagement:

The leader of the raiders, Espiñosa, was thrown from his horse early in the fight. McNelly was after him and as soon as he saw Espiñosa fall he, too, sprang to the ground. Espiñosa jumped into a "hog wallow" in the prairie and McNelly took shelter in another one. Then they fought a duel. At last McNelly played a trick on the Mexican. The Captain had a carbine and a six-shooter. He aimed his carbine carefully at the top of Espiñosa's hog wallow and then fired his pistol in the air. Espiñosa raised his head, and the next instant a bullet from McNelly's carbine had passed through it and the Mexican bandit was dead.[58]

In other accounts of this Laguna Madre or Palo Alto fight mention is made of the death and funeral of youthful ranger L. S. or "Sonny" Smith, whom the Mexican marauders killed in the engagement. There is a reference also to a costly, intricately embroidered sombrero taken from one of the Mexicans.[59]

O. Henry's portrayal of the desperado, then, it may be said in summary, seems less of an exaggeration than nature's representation of the "critter's" counterpart in the flesh. King Fisher, enig-

[58] N. A. Jennings, *op. cit.*, IX, 69.
[59] W. P. Webb, *The Texas Rangers*, XII, 247. See also, George Durham, "McNelly's Rangers", an extract from *The Inside Story of McNelly's Texas Rangers*, as published in *West* Magazine.

matical border chieftain, with his tiger-skin chaparreras, and bridle reins strung with human ears, is as unbelievable an errant from the laws of man and of God as the most extravagant invention of the fictionist. Only a writer of tragedy, in the wildest flight of imagination, would give a character such a gory end as Fisher experienced: thirteen bullet holes in head and body – and all put there with no malice aforethought in the minds of his murderers.

On February 21, 1885, Marshal Hal Gosling was shot and instantly killed by an outlaw named Yeager.[60] Gosling was bringing Yeager and his robber partner Pitts from Austin to San Antonio in a day-coach on an International train. At New Braunfels, Pitt's sister boarded the train with a basket of provisions. Gosling generously allowed the woman to offer her "goodies" to the prisoners. From the basket, the handcuffed Yeager adroitly removed a six-shooter that, presumably by chance, had been placed there with some bananas. With lightning speed the handcuffed bandit shot the good-hearted marshal dead.[61] There followed an altercation between Deputy Marshal Manning and Yeager, with Pitts an accessory to the dispute. During the disturbance Manning was wounded five times, and Pitts was so unfortunate as to get in the way of one of Manning's bullets and die as a result.

The historically-minded reader will note that Yeager, handicapped as he was by his handcuffs, made the entire complement of the six bullets of his revolver count. While this display of effectiveness could in a sense be considered a tribute to the desperado's skill, greater accuracy might have been expected from a shooter operating at such close range. Of course Marshal Manning's gun could have been a factor in Yeager's behavior.

And now a remarkable thing occurred. Yeager, with the lifeless body of his comrade in his arms and manacled to the man wrist to wrist (right or left not specified in the account), jumped out

[60] Marshal Gosling (in 1883) had received a reward of $9,730.00 for the capture of the absconding treasurer of the state of Tennessee, Marshall Tate Polk. Polk, the man with the heavy suitcases, was the person "Detective" Price let go free.

[61] San Antonio police officer John Fitz Henry, as told in a sketch of his life and experiences in the Alamo City. *Trail Drivers of Texas*, II, 827.

of the car window while the train hurried along at forty miles per hour. Out on the right-of-way, the resourceful Yeager beat to a pulp the wrist of his dead pal, freed himself, and remained at large for some days before being recaptured.[62]

Few short story writers could conjure up such fantastic and outlandish doings as Yeager's desperate acts.

If we hesitate to accept the vagaries of the absurd Calliope Catesby, we shall find the marvels of the pistol-wizardry of Ben Thompson just as hard to accept. Without any particularly undue strain on our consciences we can overlook Buck Patterson's joining with Catesby to hide from his mother the son's penchant for unlawful behavior. Calliope will deceive for a worthy cause and wear the marshal's badge only while the old lady remains in Quicksand. Thompson, however, won a permanent star after a series of pyrotechnic displays along trails of blood.

"Well, I'll mark you anyhow", said Thompson of one of his human targets who was behind a post with only his right ear protruding.[63] And the gunman fired, making a hole in the cartilage as round and as neat as if it had been put there with a punch. O. Henry, who seems to have been fascinated with this business of puncturing the right ear – he uses it three times that this chronicler knows of – endows the Llano Kid with the credibly human quality of missing his man's ear a sixteenth of an inch, the dire consequences of this human failure constituting the story that follows.[64]

And we feel, too, that it is more reasonable to suppose that Henry Ogden will free himself from the "tentacles of the law" by "alibis and other legal technicalities" than to accept the fact that President Hayes freed Ham White from a life sentence although the man had been found guilty of robbing the U. S. mails. It appears strange that Lieutenant Sandridge, the distraught lover, would throw himself down in the dust beside Tonia, his humming bird whom he has killed. But lovers of that era behaved as strangely. Kitty Leroy, a dance hall favorite, disguised herself in male

62 San Antonio *Express* (February 22, 1885).
63 Wm. W. Walton, *op. cit.*, p. 147.
64 "A Double Dyed Deceiver", *Works*, 421.

attire to fight a man who had declined to combat a woman. As they joined battle, the man fell from her well-aimed shot; she then cried over him and married him in time to be his widow.[65]

The improbability in the story of the Cisco Kid is that the wily gentleman of nefarious practices is able to dupe so successfully ranger Lieutenant Sandridge – and Mr. Alphonso Smith declares Hall's presence can be detected in Sandridge. It is certainly unlikely that a victim of such a hoax – as well as of such an unorthodox amour – would have found pleasure in recounting such unsavory details of his career to a fireside circle.

The Kid extricates himself from the trap, too, without firing a shot! No TV or western story enthusiast would tolerate a western where the bad "hombre" protagonist fails to fire his gun.

It is to be recalled also that O. Henry brings all his badman actors to the stage where he can supply them with the props and scenery he knows so well. The Cisco Kid is on the dodge from a killing he did in the Guadalupe country, but he comes to rest awhile in the grass-roofed *jacal* in a Nueces pear flat and to drink from the red earthen jar filled from a water-hole. Ham, called Black Bill, robs an M. K. & T. train north of San Antonio, but drops off the International to lie low for a spell in the chaparral sheep country. From the remarks he makes one feels that he does not think the country especially attractive – except as a place where he is unlikely to be found – or as good a hiding place as Mexico, a few miles beyond.

Calliope Catesby, embodying many of the idiosyncrasies of Ben Thompson, prefers for his gunplay the narrower sphere of Quicksand – a town pretty much on the order of Cotulla of those days. A yellow dog and a Mexican's coal-oil bottle are worthy targets for his provincial pistol.

Chicken Ruggles, the spurious Black Eagle, plays for a time with Bud King and his band of cattle and horse rustlers in the *brasada*, but the Chicken is not of their cloth. This canned oyster buccaneer and cheese pirate of colorful speech threatens for a while the supremacy of the desperado chieftain, only to fade on

[65] *Life and Adventures of Sam Bass,* p. 10.

the prospects of his first dose of lead, and make an ignominious exit.

And so do others play their parts in the chaparral. The Llano Kid finds his immediate safety in the Nueces Strip. Here Jimmy Hayes dies a hero in a hog-wallow; here the Frio Kid and King James reveal their streaks of good.

A creature of extravagant fancy, then, may we call this wayward *vaquero* of "red ruin and revenge", precursor of the ridiculous blank-pistol fisticuff travesty of radio and screen? Let us say, rather, that O. Henry's puppet badman is a truthful reflection of a creature who lived in a lawless and uncertain age.

Of him we may fittingly observe with Bud King: "I never yet see anything on the hoof that he exactly grades up with ... and he straddles a hoss from where you laid the chunk";[66] or echo the words of the Nueces Kid: "He ain't had proper trainin'. He never learned how to git skeered. Now, a man ought to be skeered enough when he tackles a fuss to hanker after readin' his name on the list of survivors, anyway." [67]

[66] "The Passing of Black Eagle", *Works*, I, 435.
[67] "An Afternoon Miracle", *Works*, 166.

XIII

JACK HARRIS'S SALOON:
THE WHOLE TO CONCLUDE WITH A TRAGEDY

Towards dusk in the evening of July 11, 1882, Frank Sparrow, Jack Harris's theatre manager, might have been observed walking down into the middle depths of the parquet of the Variety playhouse on Main Plaza. We may reasonably presume that Sparrow made such a tour of the inside of the noted playhouse since it is part of the business of theatre bosses to make sure that their houses are always in order for the entertainment of the day. Walking about here and there and glancing up and down Sparrow certainly could have done so with a feeling of satisfaction. His eye could presently have come to rest on an enormous chandelier of scintillating pendants which shone with brilliance on the new folding chairs that surrounded him on all sides. He doubtlessly ascended the stairs to inspect the half-hidden nooks in the out-of-way places roundabout the "circle". In this area refreshment parlors had been provided for patrons wishing the comparative quiet these curtained recesses afforded. In a house where the clientele were generally reputed to be of an unquiet disposition it is natural to suppose that sensitive patrons would often desire the comforting seclusion of these "parlors".

The proscenium boxes were now declared by the city press to be as "neat" as those of the larger and more genteel theatres of the city. New machinery had been installed under the stage, mechanical contraptions that made possible the presentation of "sensation" acts, such as steamboat explosions and "transformations". Billy Sims, managerial assistant, had engaged for the coming season an entirely new company of selected stars from the vaudeville theatres of Chicago, Cincinnati, and Saint Louis. "Thirteen young ladies, tastefully attired, swing to and fro, in suspension – in the swinging first part", so the bills said. While one might not find it especially startling to observe *one* fine lady swinging "in suspension", to see thirteen of these beauties, and tastefully attired to boot, all taking the air at one time, is something little short of a marvel.

The star of the aggregation of performers was the charming Miss Kitty Wells, called "the pearl of the variety stage". Another performer was Miss Maud Walker, a dashing serio-comic vocalist. Gertie Harrington was a third songstress; and Jennie Mason was written up in the bills as a balladist of "no inconsiderable talent". Frank Lester was presented in his original absurdity entitled "Freaks", a specialty replete with song and dance and flashes of wit. Miss Maggie Mauri would do a clog dance with Hans Michel accompanying her "on bones". Then there were Mason and Ralston, blackface comedians, with their plantation sketch. Mason was six feet six inches "high", and "Major" Ralston was a Lilliputian who measured twenty-six inches in length. Quite frequently in the course of their humorous dialogue (a laugh-provoking act of top quality), the Major would walk between the legs of the more elevated Mason.[1]

The whole was to conclude with a farce.

Such in substance was the "olio" at the Variety theatre during the second week of July, 1882. But poor Jack Harris, about to exhale his last breath of life, was to see none of the entertainment on that fatal evening of July 11, 1882. Just a few minutes before curtain-time, Ben Thompson, city marshal of Austin, fired two shots with his .44 calibre pistol into the body of the genial theatre proprietor and saloon-keeper, and dropped that worthy gentleman to the ground mortally wounded. When shot, Harris was standing behind a louvred shutter that half hid him from the view of his antagonist. Those two shots were heard clean from the Paso del Norte to Sabine Pass. The door figuring in the tragedy opened both into the drinking establishment and onto the stairs leading up to the Variety Theatre, a notable Santone amuse-

---

[1] San Antonio *Evening Light* (September 21, 1882).

ment center in the 70's and 80's. Just previous to the fatal shots, Thompson had asked his intended victim, "What are you going to do with that shot gun, you damned s— of a b——h?" This query has always struck the narrator as being one of the most remarkable instances of irony in the annals of unconventional gun-play. Of course Ben knew what Jack was going to do with his shotgun. As irrelevant as the question was, Thompson is reported to have asked it. Following the interrogatory, Harris, we are told, paused for a moment (possibly to reflect on the many uncertainties of life), and then retorted, "To shoot you, you d——d s–on of a b——h." [2]

Aside from a lack of originality at repartee, Harris could be censured for his hesitancy in recognizing the urgent need of hoisting his piece of ordinance into a position for a telling shot at his challenger; as a result of this reflective pause, the former U. S. Mormon War scout suffered the fatal consequences above narrated. In justice to Harris, however, we feel obliged to say that he probably thought that, concealed as he was behind the shutters, he was not giving a too clear imitation of a target. But why on earth (some may think) had this fiery Texan armed himself with a shotgun? Why was he not armed with one of Mr. Sam Colt's ingenious revolving pistols of a large calibre, like a .44 or a .45? Had not Jack Hays, June Walker, and the two Gillespies shown how deadly the six-shot handgun could be in the hands of a top-marksman? [3] Indulgent reader, Mr. Harris was not a Texan. He was a Connecticut-born Yankee, a lineal descendant on his mother's side of Israel Putnam, and at the time of his decease his mother was living on the Putnam farm (in said state of Connecticut) from money sent her from San Antonio by her son Jack. [4] That Jack had earned the money at the gaming table and from the sales of ardent spirits to delinquents and disreputable vagrants was more of a coincidence than a deliberate intention. Whatever we may say of the nature of Jack's professional pursuits

---

[2] *Ibid.* (July 12, 1882).
[3] For the exploits of these early Texan Rangers, see (among other sources) Samuel C. Reid, Jr., *The Scouting Expeditions of McCulloch's Texas Rangers.*
[4] San Antonio *Evening Light* (July 12, 1882).

we could hardly believe that these ventures were not attended with some risk.

Harris had explained a few days prior to his tragic end, in reply to a question put to him by an inquisitive friend, that Thompson was such a lowdown cuss that he was fit to be killed only with slugs or heavy shot thrown at him by a full-choke or scatter-bore. The curious gentleman then had questioned the effectiveness of a "fowling-piece" as a dueling weapon, and had heard Harris retort that, "I can kill a bird flying. Why should I not be able to kill a man standing?"[5] Poor Jack. It was a pity he came to such an ignoble end. He ought to have known that Thompson's irascible nature would not permit him to give a rival a fair show.

It is a mite ironical in a way that Ben Thompson, who began his gunman career with an old double-barreled Sheffield twelve gauge fowling piece, and had once in Abilene, Kansas, given such a masterly proof of the muzzle-energy of this weapon – it is just a trifle ironical that such a man would have elected to carry his attack to Harris with a .44 calibre handgun. We can only infer that he was induced to make his choice of weapon because of an awareness of his skill as an off-hand shot with a pistol.[6] It was nothing for Ben, without half trying, to shoot an underbit or overbit – or even a half-crop – on an offending party's ear. "I'll just put my brand on you", he was wont to remark. And then he would proceed to perform the act.

After firing the two deadly shots into the corporeal frame of proprietor Harris, Thompson discharged another shot into the air to discourage whatever other conspirators who might be lurking about (he is thought to have declared); this business done, he issued forth from the building by the west door; and (as rumor had it) waved his pistol playfully towards Professor F. G. Hyworth and his musicians. The professor was with his band on

5   *Ibid.* (July 13, 1882).
6   The writer of course knows that the Harris-Thompson contest embraced none of the traits of a formal duel. As for the employment of shotguns as weapons in duels, see Major Ben C. Truman, *The Field of Honor*, XXII; and *passim.*

the balcony above the theatre-entrance, as was his daily custom, rendering popular airs before curtain-time. The professor and his group, it is reported, were so engrossed with the rendition of the evening overture that Ben's shot into the air failed to disturb them. A bystander whose identity was not determined was later to declare that the musicians were offering their version of a well-known overture by a German opera composer. In view of the tragic incident but a moment before taking place within the doors of the entertainment hall, one would hardly deduce that this composition could have been Beethoven's *Consecration of the House*, Opus 124. The same observer just referred to remarked likewise that Ben appeared cheerful as he leisurely made his way across Main Plaza and entered at once into the dazzling brilliancy of the vestibule of Fowler and Berliner's popular White Elephant Saloon. Within the public resort he is reported to have bought a fifteen-cent *colorado claro* Henry Clay cigar, and glanced into what was fittingly termed by the proprietors of the bar as the "deepest room" in the city. The genial peace-officer's eyes could have rested for a moment on the eight billiard tables that occupied the lower half of this spacious room – but just for a moment – no longer perhaps than to reflect on what a handsome addition these permanent adjuncts would be to his own rooms at Austin – and then he walked briskly over the tessellated blocks of white and black marble till he stopped at the bar itself. This fixture was a massive mahogany object of rare elegance. Ben did not seem in the least affected at the sight of the pyramids of gleaming crystal reflected with splendid brightness in the French plate glass mirror beyond. At the bar, he was joined by his brother Billy (whom on several occasions he had been obliged to retrieve from embarrassment), and after partaking of a light spirituous stimulant, the two brothers on Ben's suggestion left the White Elephant and began slowly to wend their way eastward down Commerce Street to the Menger Hotel. On the day following, Ben Thompson, as only a conscientious peace-officer could, surrendered to Sheriff (of Bexar county) McGall and City Marshal (of San Antonio) Shardien.

Thompson's biographer, Buck Walton, says that Ben was born

in Nottingly, Yorkshire, England.[7] The date of his birth, I believe, is given as 1842, or thereabouts. Although Thompson's father was a sea captain, the son appears to have found the thin dry ozone of the hinterland of Texas more suited to his means than the salt air of the seven seas. The young adventurer fought Indians in West Texas, had somewhat of a spotty record as a Confederate soldier, and later tried his hand in the fortunes of the ill-fated Maximillian in Mexico.

For a time in Thompson's surprising career the man served as city marshal of Austin. As a peace-officer, Ben fulfilled his duties in a creditable fashion. Some year or so after his demise an Austin newspaper spoke of the marshal in praiseworthy terms. The journal cited as an instance of lawlessness an amorous couple riding down the Avenue, kissing and hugging in plain view of amazed law-abiding onlookers. "When Ben Thompson was marshal no such lawless behavior would have been tolerated", the newspaper commented. Thompson was living proof of the adage (referred to once in a while by O. Henry in capsule portraits of many of his errant creatures) that there's a bit of good in the worst of us. The marshal, we must concede, may sometimes have misinterpreted an evil impulse for a good. He is credited for instance with saying that he killed Jack Harris because the ex-soldier was corrupting the morals of the young men of San Antonio.

As a badman Thompson had gained a state-wide notoriety. After his fracas with Harris it was months before a San Antonio judge could select a jury to try him. Of Ben it could be said truly that his life was an open book; and there was hardly a man in Texas who did not know every page – nay, every paragraph of that book. Hence it was almost impossible to find a man who had not made up his mind about Thompson's innocence or guilt in the Harris case. At last a venire drew in a backswoodsman who had never heard of the pistol wizard! The *Express* gave this curious "critter" a much-deserved write-up in its columns. The case finally did go to trial on January 21, 1883. (On January 17

[7] W. M. Walton, *Life of Ben Thompson*, Chapters XIII and XIV.

a flaw in the indictment had been cited: the phrase, "Ben Thompson killed Jack Harris", was changed to read, "Ben Thompson killed a man commonly known as Jack Harris." This would seem to have been a point in favor of the defendant.) On the 23rd at ten A. M. the jury returned a verdict of "not guilty". The *Express* reported that a large crowd has assembled in the court-room for the event, and that "public sentiment was divided" as to the prisoner's guilt.[8]

A little more than a year after his acquittal, while the former peace-officer was recreating himself during Mardi Gras week in Galveston, the *Daily News* of that city (then the metropolis of Texas) carried an account of an interview which a reporter of the journal had had with Thompson. Since the article throws light on the character of the man, it may not be amiss to present a bit of its substance here.

After telling the newspaper representative something of his career in Texas while in the Confederate service, and as a soldier under the Emperor Maximillian, Thompson laughed when he said, "You newspaper fellows make a target of me, whenever you get short of an item, and magnify my proportions, until actually timid people will cross to the other side of the street rather than meet that bad man Ben Thompson." [9]

Ben went on to say that what the public prints said about him he found amusing. He knew the ways of news folk because he had worked as a printer himself for a number of newspapers, including the *State-Times* [of Austin], when that journal was run by Rip Ford and Joe Walker.

"Now, since I've been here [in Galveston] five days, I don't think anybody can say that I've done anything horrible; do you?"

And of course any of his listeners would have to admit that

---

[8] The lawyers for the prosecution, as listed by the *Evening Light* of January 23, 1883, were District Attorney Cocke; Messrs. Tarleton and Brown, Messrs. T. G. and G. Anderson, Judge Devine, Trevanion T. Teel, and W. R. Wallace. For the defence there were W. M. (Buck) Walton, who was also Thompson's biographer; Messrs. Hill and Wooten, and Pendexter of Austin; and Messrs. John A. and N. O. Green, Jr., of San Antonio.

[9] The Galveston *Daily News* (March 3, 1884).

what he said was true. When asked about his proficiency as a marksman, Ben said that he prided himself on his accuracy with gun or pistol.

"You have heard it said that I wear a steel mask." [He evidently meant a breast-plate.] "Now look at me."

To prove the truth if his remark, he bared his breast and back, revealing as he did so a "silk-thread" undershirt.

He had come down to Galveston, he said, to enjoy the Mardi Gras season and had "taken in" an operatic concert which presented the celebrated diva, Minnie Hauk. "I went to hear Minnie Hauk sing, and I just think she 's immense. If it had just been in English, I would have liked it much more." [10]

Actually, enjoying the Mardi Gras was merely a side issue with Ben. He explained that he had really come down to the Gulf coast area to see about buying a ranch at Clear Lake. He was tired of his turbulent life and hoped to be let alone when he went into the stock-raising business, let alone "by the newspapers, and all busy-bodies, as well as the other people".

The newsman could not restrain an urge to ask the Austin peace-officer a really pertinent question before the interview ended:

"Mr. Thompson, how many difficulties have you taken part in?" [11]

Ben showed a reluctance to discuss the matter by lighting a cigar and calling for drinks.

Thompson, like a city of varied racial composition and many

[10] Minnie Hauk (1852-1929), the Baroness de Wartegg, was an American-born prima donna. She made her début as the "Wonder Child" of sixteen in New York in 1868, in the rôle of Amina in *La Sonnambula*; her European début was at Paris the following year, in the same rôle. Minnie Hauk retired in 1886 and lived her remaining years with her husband at their estate at Tribschen on Lake Lucerne in Switzerland. The diva made occasional appearances in favorite rôles until 1895.

[11] The term "difficulty" has a connotation that younger people today perhaps do not understand. The word was usually applied to an informally conducted contest between forces, usually men, in which side-arms were generally employed by one or both of the involved parties, said arms being used to gain the desired "satisfaction." Mark Twain writes of "An Arkansaw Difficulty" in *Huckleberry Finn*.

degrees of wealth, was an infinity of contradictions. He was a man of paradoxes. He was a peace-officer, and yet a desperado. He was a loving husband and father, yet was not averse to making widows and orphans. He was English born, yet he went in the catalog for a Texas badman. He could mulct an innocent man of his honestly won dollars, yet he would be the last man in the world to rob a train or stage-coach. He could sit peacefully and enjoy an operatic performance; with the same degree of satisfaction he could spend long hours at the faro table. He could make plans on the third of March to settle down to raising cattle and horses, yet a week later he became involved in a contention that sent him to his grave with eleven bullet-holes in his body. Unquestionably, Ben Thompson was a man of contrarieties. And so was Jack Harris, the unfortunate victim of the Austin marshal's aggression. Who would have expected to find a descendant of Israel Putnam running a drinking-bar and vaudeville theatre in San Antonio, Texas, in the eighties? Yet that is precisely what Harris was doing when he met his death. Besides that, he was a political boss who could deliver an appreciable number of votes to a favored candidate, provided that candidate was a Democrat. Jack, who should of course have been a Yankee, and a Puritan to boot, openly professed no liking for the Yankee breed. Shortly after returning from his last visit to his widowed mother he had told a *Light* newsman of his distaste for Yankees. The fact that he had lost a hand in the Confederate service seems to have discolored his view of carpetbaggers. Many of these latter accused Jack of controlling the "sporting fraternity", and of corrupting the morals of the young people of San Antonio. (Ben Thompson pretended to nourish such a notion as this, too, but many suspected that Ben was really irked because Jack had won a heap of money from him in poker games.)

The fickleness of Harris's erstwhile political associates, many of whom where deeply indebted to the man, drew a comment from the *Light* newspaper at the time of his death. The journal had noted the absence at the funeral of Harris's "friends" of many years. It quoted a few lines of poetry which it apparently thought suitable for the occasion:

And what is friendship but a name,
A charm that lulls to sleep,
A sound that follows wealth and fame,
And leaves the wretch to weep.

So much for Harris. Let us consign his memory to the footnotes of history. We must now return to Thompson for a comment on the Galveston interview.

The most startling bit of news that came to light in the interview of Thompson by the Galveston newsman was Ben's declaration that he had really "come down" to buy a ranch at Clear Lake, where he hoped to settle down and be let alone by the newspapers. Yes, in a measure it startles a body to read that this fiery-tempered genius would ever have entertained the idea of giving up the daring practices that had gained him notoriety from Doan's Store to Point Isabel. But such was the declared intention of this erratic figure, on the first of March, 1884. How are we to interpret this notice of his wish to return to a quiet nook of the Clear Lake region to engage in some form of pastoral pursuit, possibly the raising of beef cattle? Regardless of his sincerity (and this chronicler is of no disposition to question Ben's possession of this quality), it is doubtful whether the marshal's impetuous nature would have enabled him to shuffle off the life of hurry and bustle which he had for so long a time been disposed to pursue. We are therefore not particularly surprised to read in the public prints of March eleventh of the Austin peace-officer's violent death the day before. The sad event had taken place at Jack Harris's old stand, the Variety Theatre of San Antonio, shortly before midnight. Ben had returned to Austin from his visit to the coast and again taken up the business that seemed so well suited to his tastes, to wit, gambling. His biographer reports that Ben appeared to be in a gayer mood than usual on the day that was to mark the end of his earthly career; as was a custom of his, honored fairly well in the observance, he had imbibed rather freely of ardent spirits.[12] It chanced likewise that on the very day which was to be Ben's last on this earth, John King Fisher, sometime border

---

[12] W. M. Walton, *op. cit.*, Chapter XXV.

cowman and horse-trader, but at that time deputy-sheriff of Uvalde county, had come to the Capital City on a "fence-cutting" mission. Somehow the two notables got together. As rumor had it, they were several hours "taking in the town". In the afternoon, the men quietly boarded on International train for San Antonio. Ben indulged in many frivolities during the journey. The train porter seems to have been the butt of some of the Marshal's sportive abuse. This dusky functionary is reported to have been kept in a constant state of agitation all the way from the Capital City to Santone.

Thompson's biographer indicates that his subject had to be persuaded to board the train at the last minute; partisans of Fisher say that the deputy-sheriff disliked the Marshal and tolerated him only because he could not escape his presence.[13] It is a historian's conjecture as to what really prompted the two officers to travel together, but we do know that they arrived in San Antonio at eight o'clock P. M. and appear to have gone soon thereafter to the Turner Opera House. This amusement place, then serving the city as its chief theatre, stood on Houston street, one door east of St. Mary's.

The play of the evening was the popular eye-moistener, *East Lynne*, with Ada Gray in the rôle of Mrs. Henry Wood's popular but erring heroine, Lady Isabel Carlyle (nee Vine). Ada Gray, a Boston-born actress, had done Shakespearean parts with both John Wilkes and Edwin Booth. For a number of years she had devoted a good part of her time to *Camille* and *East Lynne*. The San Antonio *Express*, on the momentous occasion of which we treat, had found the actress "thoroughly conversant with the character of Lady Isabel Vine . . . and effective and natural in the scene with her dying child". The paper was referring of course to the scene where the grieving Lady Isabel, in the guise of Madame Vine, returns to the Carlyle home in time to hold in her arms as he dies her little consumptive son William. Thompson, as we learn from Buck Walton, had developed a fondness for Miss Gray from seeing her perform on her frequent visits to Millet's

---

[13]   *Ibid.*, Chapters XXV and XXVI.

Main Plaza, San Antonio. Jack Harris's Saloon in Right Background.

The Vaudeville Theatre,

W. H. SIMMS, General Manager.

Sumptuous Repast for March 10, 11, 12

The whole to begin with the acknowledged.
Prince of humor, FRANK RICE in
his mirth provoking extravaganza, entitled

"VOT I CAN DO."

Assisted by our corps of perfection.

Music vs. muscle. Our Lone Star orchestra.

Part II—our olio of pleasant surprises, led by
the peerless songstress,

MISS LIZZIE MACK

Followed by the vivacious, graceful and
talented specialists—MISS MAY SMITH.

Supplemented by the mogul of fun—CHARLIE
FRYE—in his original specialty

THE CANIBALISTIC ZOUAVE.

Then we have the exceedingly meritorious
cantatrice—MISS MILLIE DAVENPORT.

Quickly succeeded by the charming MISS
JOSIE SIMMONS, in a bouquet of melody.

FRANK RICE—in his Anglo Saxony-Fizee-
Island specialty.

The voluptuous sero-comic—MISS JENNIE
HOWARD.

For the first time in this city, the great East
India

NAUTCH DANCERS.

M'lle Farina, M'lle Euphremia, M'lle Claribello,
M'lle Cazalacca.

The most laughable ethiopian absurdity extant

SKIDIKADINKADOO !

Skidika, Charlie Frye; Dinkadoo, Ed Sylvester.
And then the band played.

Once more to the front—MISS LIZZIE MACK.

The transcendently beautiful vocal duo, the

SMITH SISTERS,

Kitty and May, in captivating melange of
melody, A veritable combination of loveli-
ness, grace and vocal refinement,

By request, Mr. Charles Frye will sing the
baso-profundo solo, THE OLD SEXTON,
Particular attention is called to the depth
and flexibility of this gentleman's voice,

MISS MILLIE DAVENPORT will again oblige.

Our ever-welcome Son of Momus, ED SYL-
VESTER, with a knap-sack full of fun.

MISS JOSIE SIMMONS.

Once more, the $10,000 beauty, FRANK RICE,
the most handsome man in the world—from
his feet down.

A few minutes more with the sprightly Miss
JENNIE HOWARD.

Miss KITTIE SMITH, in her recherche specialties.

Overture, Wait for the Afterpiece, Orchestra.

Our mammoth entertainment will close with
the side-splitting, uprorious afterpiece,
(by Charlie Frye) entitled,

ASSASSINATION

Or, The Night Owls of Alamo Plaza.

Ready Bob, }
Tim Timidity, } Outlaws. { Charlie Frye
{ Ed Sylvester

Other characters by the company.

Olio, at Vaudeville Theatre,
March 1884.

opera house in Austin, and probably had been induced on that account to view her performance at Turner Hall in San Antonio.

As to how Marshal Thompson found this talented emotionalist on that fateful night, we can only surmise. Colonel Walton has left no record of the man's impressions of the play. We do know that Thompson still harbored a wish for further entertainment after the show – entertainment of a lighter vein, we may say; and urged on by such a feeling, he prevailed upon Fisher to accompany him on a visit to the Harris Variety theatre on Main Plaza. The celebrated place of amusement was now under the direction of Billy Sims, assisted by Joe Foster, neither of whom could be said to enjoy the friendship of Ben Thompson. King Fisher, we learn, was on good terms with the proprietors and even felt himself under obligation to Foster for the latter's display of kindness on a particular occasion.[14]

The olio at the Theatre that night was notable for its variety. The "sumptuous repast" (for March 10, 11, 12) featured Frank Rice, "prince of humor", in an extravaganza called "Vot I Can Do". Charley Frye, billed as a mogul of fun, was presenting his original specialty, "The Cannibalistic Zouave". Besides the cantatrices, Josie Simmons and Millie Davenport, in a bouquet of melody, there was (for the first time in the city) the "great East India NAUTCH DANCERS: Mlle. Farina, Mlle. Euphremia, Mlle. Claribello, and Mlle. Cazalacca".[15] This exotic Terpsichorean demonstration was followed by a "mirth-provoking" Ethiopean absurdity, entitled SKIDIKADINKADOO. The whole was to conclude with Charlie Frye's uproarious afterpiece, under the title of ASSASSINATION, *or The Night Owls of Alamo Plaza*.

Thompson and Fisher entered this "den of infamy" (as Ben's

[14] Foster was said to have sent meals to Fisher once while the latter was detained in the Bexar county jail at San Antonio. This instance of kindness took place long before Fisher had been elected to the office of deputy sheriff; and the offence for which he was held was a minor one.

[15] *Nautch*, an Indian ballet-dance. The *nautch* is performed by nautch-girls who scarcely move their feet, and the dance consists of swaying and posturing with the arms. *Encyclopedia Britannica* (1947), XVI, 166. Also: *Nautch*; notch, na (t) ch. 1. An East Indian exhibition of dancing, performed by professional dancing girls. *The Shorter Oxford Dictionary* (1959).

Boswell, W. M. Walton called the Variety Theatre), had drinks at the bar, engaged in a somewhat jovial but restrained conversation with Billy Sims, general manager, and were presently invited upstairs by that kindly gentleman to witness the vaudeville performance. The two peace-officers accepted the invitation, and proceeded leisurely to seats in the upper tiers. The house was crowded, with no other seats available.

Once seated the men ordered more drinks, and Thompson, enlivened a great deal by the spirits he had previously imbibed, kept on asking for Joe Foster.

"Where's Joe Foster?" he would say. "I want to square things with Joe Foster. Bring him up."

All the time, of course, Ben, by reason of his devilish, revengeful nature, actually fancied he had a score to settle with Foster. Sims after a while, with the purpose, it is alleged, of making Foster and Thompson friends, sent a messenger to tell his assistant to come up. When Foster arrived, he is reported to have refused to shake hands with Thompson, some of the former's friends averring that he felt that he could not conscientiously shake the hand of the man who had killed his friend Jack Harris just twenty months before. (As a modified disciple of Ben Thompson, the author cannot help but admire Foster for his loyalty to his departed associate. Many modern politicians would do well to make Foster a pattern for their guidance.)

The San Antonio *Light* published a different version of Ben's rencontre with Foster. When Ben asked Foster to have a drink with him, the latter (according to *The Light*) simply said, "You know, Ben, I wouldn't drink." [16] And when the marshal invited him to shake hands with him, Foster said that he would not shake because Ben had mistreated *him*! Such a statement would indicate that Foster was more concerned with ideas of personal abuse than with respect to the memory of his late friend, Jack Harris.

Ben was at once furious with Foster for his attitude and cried out with some force: "God damn you! I'm glad you won't drink or shake hands with me!"

[16] San Antonio *Evening Light* (March 11, 1884).

The theatre police-officer, a man named Coy (says *The Light*) at this moment intervened and asked Thompson to leave the building. Thompson is reported to have ordered Coy out of his way, and to have followed up this command by calling Foster a thief and making a vile reference to a female dog, which last remark he accompanied by a vigorous slap on Foster's cheek.

It is claimed by some that officer Coy at this point grabbed Thompson's revolver by the cylinder to keep the Austin marshal from discharging the weapon at Foster. Biographer Walton records no such detail. And certain it is that both Thompson and Fisher were presently thereafter standing far enough away from Sims, Foster, and Coy to receive the full brunt of a volley of pistol shots fired into and upon them, at point blank range. Hidden assailants fired the shots. Thompson received five bullets in his head and four in his body. Fisher had thirteen bullet holes in his face and body. Before he was shot down, Thompson did succeed in shattering Foster's leg and grazing Coy's body.

The Austin *Daily Satesman* was to report that "dissolute women with blanched faces" crowded round the fallen bodies, exclaiming wildly, half-choked with sobs: "Which is Ben? Show me Ben! Is that him?"

The *Statesman* reporter when in San Antonio would of course see the feminine performers at the "Theatre" as wantons, for it had been the marshal's contention that Jack Harris made a living from prostitutes. That had been Ben's professed reason for killing the former Morman-War scout, as the reader may recall. There is of course no solid basis for the assumption that girl vaudeville performers – even the "ponies" who went about among the patrons vending drinks – were necessarily "crooked". As Eddie Foy said of such women in the amusement houses of Dodge City, most were widows and abandoned wives who were as straight as deaconesses; they had often been forced to adopt their profession because of the perfidy of the men whom they had once trusted.[17]

Be all that as it may, it certainly appears likely that hidden assassins caused the death of Thompson and Fisher. Nine slug-

---

[17]   Eddie Foy and Alvin F. Harlow, *Clowning Trough Life*, Chap. X.

holes in the one and thirteen in the other are unquestionable instances that support such a contention. Another indisputable fact is that the passing of these two errant and uncontrollable spirits caused the greatest sensation in Texas since the victory of San Jacinto. Papers all over the state were filled with dispatches about the murders; editorial pens were busied with appraisals of the two principals involved in the tragic act in which they made their last bow. Men of prominence from the Red River to the Rio Grande were queried by reporters as to their opinions of Ben. Columns in the public prints were filled for days with stories of the former Austin marshal.

The bodies of both victims were soon laid to rest in their respective home cities, Austin and Uvalde, and quiet thereafter reigned in that turbulent otherworld in which bad men and good, who set not their lives above a pin's fee, were often more ready to settle differences in the chambers of firearms than in those of a court of law.

In the Proem to *Cabbages and Kings*, O. Henry makes the Carpenter say that "it shall be a duty and a pleasing sport to wander
with Momus beneath the tropic stars where Melpomene once
stalked austere". And later, the Carpenter adds "there is a little
tale to tell . . . and in it there are indeed shoes and ships and
sealing-wax and cabbage-palms and presidents instead of kings".
In a sense these words, with modification, are applicable to the
Southwest stories; for in the latter the author does indeed revel in
the kind of absurdity and nonsense that Lewis Carroll (Charles
Lutwidge Dodgson) manages so well in the Alice books. Whereas
Dodgson attained his effects through the clever handling of sym-
bols in such stuff as dreams are made of, O. Henry achieved his
ends with playful exaggeration through a deft manipulation of
plot, with little droll touches here and there, to advance the progress of the scene and set off character.

There is something about "Hostages to Momus" that puts us
in mind at once of episodes in the Alice books.[1] The two works
have points of resemblance both in flavor and in substance. In
the beginning of "Hostages to Momus" we meet Tecumseh Pickens
and Caligula Polk right after they have incurred the displeasure
of President Porfirio Diaz by conducting a lottery and monte
game in Tamaulipas, Mexico. The two gentlemen hike out for the
Texas border with the *rurales* in hot pursuit at their heels. (Pickens
describes the *rurales* as something like our Supreme Court mounted
on broncos and armed with Winchesters.) "Pick" and Polk soon

[1] "Hostages to Momus", *Works*, I, 337.

take refuge in a brickyard at Matamoras and at night swim the Rio Grande, Polk so agitated with fear that he crosses the stream absentmindedly with a brick in each hand.[2]

The Hatter, as first witness in the trial of the Knave of Hearts before the Judge-King of Hearts, is so uneasy and nervous because of the Queen's hard stare at him that he bites a large piece from the rim of his tea cup, which object said Hatter has rather incongruously brought into court with him.[3]

Still fleeing, Pick and Caligula "migrate" through San Antonio to New Orleans; and after an experience in the "otherworld" of the latter city, board a train for parts then unknown to them. Pick later declares that he has an insufficient recollection of buying two yellow tickets through a window, of hearing a man say, "All aboard", and of the "butcher" covering him and Caligula with figs and the works of Augusta Jane Evans.[4]

Alice, in the Looking-Glass World, finds herself in a railway carriage, with a guard looking in at a window and demanding tickets, which objects she has neglected to buy because she does not know why she is on the train, and does not "belong to the railway journey at all".[5]

Alice has her experience with the live flowers and Looking Glass insects.[6] Pick and Polk, after their train trip (which they make as if in a dream) and when they become "revised", are awakened from a night's sleep in a little pine hotel by the "noise of flowers and the smell of birds". Alice might wonder at the speech of the Tiger-lily and the Rose and at the sight of the Bread-and-butter fly, but the sound that Pick and Polk hear is merely that of sunflowers banging against the wall by the force of the wind. The smell of the birds proves to be the odor of a chicken-coop beneath their bedroom window.[7]

Polk's question to the hotel proprietor, while not couched exactly in Jabberwocky words, is, we must confess, slightly cryptic.

[2] *Ibid.*, 337, 338.
[3] Lewis Carroll, *Alice's Adventures in Wonderland*, XI, 168.
[4] "Hostages to Momus", *Works*, I, 338.
[5] Lewis Carroll, *Through the Looking Glass*, III, 48-54.
[6] *Ibid.*, II, III.
[7] "Hostages to Momus", *op. cit.*, I, 338.

"Would you mind telling us why we are at?" he asks. "We know the reason we are where, but can't exactly figure out on account of what place." [8]

These words may be puzzling to a reader, but they are readily understood by the hotel man. He had observed that the two guests had come in drunk and quickly tells them that they are in Mountain Valley, Georgia.

When the white Rabbit-Herald reads the anonymous verses, both the King and Queen declare that the lines incriminate the Knave. As we can see by one of the stanzas, Alice's statement that there's not a jot of sense in the lines seems perfectly true. The assurance of their Majesties does not seem justified. The stanza follows:

> I gave her one, they gave him two,
>   You gave us three or more;
> They all returned from him to you,
>   Though they were mine before.

The King tries his luck at an analysis of the verses, but runs into trouble when he reaches the word "fit". [9]

Alice wakes up from her dream of wonders to find her head in her sister's lap, with dead leaves gently falling down upon her from the trees above them. [10] Pick and Calig., as Messrs. Pickens and Polk are facetiously called, with their frightening experience in Mexico as an inciting force, flee as in a dream through Santone and New Orleans and wake from a state of intoxication and sleep at a small hotel in Mountain Valley. They both then set about to create a world of fantasy into which they trap Colonel Jackson T. Rockingham. The two grafters plan to collect a ransom for the release of this man, the president of the Sunrise and Edenville Tap Railroad. The illusion pops like a bubble and brings the schemers back to a sense of reality when they discover that their impoverished victims have turned tables on them to enjoy the elaborate hoax at the expense of the perpetrators. As matters de-

---

[8] *Ibid.*
[9] *Alice's Adventures in Wonderland*, XII, 186.
[10] *Ibid.*, 189.

velop, the railroad officials have large stomachs to fill rather than large purses to empty.

In his Southwest stories, O. Henry shows a fondness for the Humpty Dumpty word, a device now and then of perhaps questionable effectiveness as a source of amusement. The Humpty Dumpty word, as Lewis Carroll's character of that name explains to Alice, is a word invested with as many meanings as its user wants to give it. Humpty Dumpty shows what he means by explaining his rather wide use of "Impenetrability".[11] None of O. Henry's stories is more generously supplied with these Humpty Dumpty extravagancies of diction than "Hostages to Momus". As instances in proof, we cite a number: "cotton bales", as an adjunct to female beauty; "amenable in the exercise" of sentiments; an "edifice" of pound cake and "flexible" sandstone; "mahogany" for hog and hominy; "edifying" referring to a dinner; "infatuated with ramifications" of specified articles of food; "permeate" along the sidewalks; "immoral function" and "derogatory list"; "inartistic" to the stomach; board of "perforation and . . . depravity"; "inoculate the occasion"; eat in haste like a "grammarian".

"Calig's" use of "demitasse" for "demirep" is a satisfactory malapropism, but "conniseer" for "connoisseur" would seem merely to be on the order of a country bumpkin's mistake.[12]

Other Southwest stories of course furnish examples of characters making words mean what they want them to, but the samples offered above seem sufficiently illustrative of the practice. There is, however, one further instance that it might be well to quote: Baldy Woods, when telling Webster Yeager of the latter's prince-consort status, suggests that he "start a interregnum or a habeas corpus".[13] Humpty Dumpty himself could not have done better.

So much has been said elsewhere in this work of O. Henry's contrivances and schemes for creating humorous effects that the study can perhaps be brought profitably to an end with a few random additions.

[11]   *Through the Looking Glass*, VI, 124, 125.
[12]   "Hostages to Momus", *op. cit.*, 337-347.
[13]   "Hearts and Crosses", *op cit.*, I, 109.

"The Ethics of Pig", the last story of *The Gentle Grafter* series, and the story best calculated to "tickle the risibilities" of the reader, is replete with Humpty Dumpty words (witness "propitious", and "ambiguous blue eyes"); curious twists (like "dinkus-thrower" and "non-actionable thriftiness"); and outlandish or "metaphysical" conceits (such as "Tuskegee ... tan" color, and "unlettered hinds"); all of these delicacies are neatly woven into a closely-knit framework and given lustre by a well-greased action.[14]

"The Ethics of Pig" looks very much as if it were built on a variation of the "cheater-cheated" plot, but the story could have been inspired by tall-tales recounted of the malicious behavior of Mississippi steamboat gamblers. As a case in support of this latter assumption, we may cite a story told of Bill Walker, notorious river-boat gamester. On an occasion Bill boarded a "down" boat at Memphis, disguised as a minister of the gospel. His demure manner and innocent expression immediately drew the attention of a brace of small-fry sharpsters or "beats". Walker of course allowed himself to fall a victim to the wiles of these seductive creatures.

"Poker? My goodness, what is that, please tell me?" Walker said, in response to an invitation to join his new acquaintances in a "little game".

"And these cards with faces and spots on 'em? Are these what you use in your little game?"

The two spiders smiled to observe the unwary clergyman becoming so thoroughly enmeshed. But "long ere the play was played" the fly had assumed all the manners of a wasp. As a consequence of the metamorphosis, never were two would-be "cony-catchers" themselves so roundly "catched".[15]

In O. Henry's story, grafter Jefferson Peters, one of the author's wittiest and cleverest creations, is "taken in" completely by a Mount Nebo rustic whom he had sized up as eminently acceptable as a trustworthy partner in a shell game. As the story begins Jeff

---

[14]   "The Ethics of Pig", *op. cit.*, I, 347.
[15]   The sketch of gambler Bill Walker is based on material from an undated item in *The New York Clipper* in the files of the Harvard Theatre Collection.

tells how he quietly drifted into the North Carolina village thinking surely that if an "honest" partner for his "unillegal graft" could be found it would be here in Mount Nebo. After sojourning in the hamlet long enough to convince the citizens that he is not a "reve-nuer", he hears about and soon thereafter makes the acquaintance of Rufe Tatum. Rufe has just ended a thirty-day sentence in the town jail for killing a fellow townsman named Yance Goodloe, but in his interview with Jeff, Rufe confesses to the greater crime of hog-stealing. This "shoat-lifter" has a readiness of tongue that seems more consonant with the character of a sophisticate than that of a Rube. But Jeff sees him as a Rube, and dressing him to suit the part carries him down into the lowlands to be capper in a shell-game. On his first test, Rufe disappoints Jeff by not appear-ing to assume his role as capper. Later it is shown that the Mount Nebo expert has been out plying his craft again and has a fine shoat on hand as proof of the success of his night's venture. Jeff finds this out and upbraids the fellow severely for his indiscretion and leaves him to go to bed. In the morning Jeff is startled to find a notice in a Lexington newspaper offering a $5000 reward for an educated pig stolen from a circus showing in the city.

A veritable battle of wits then takes place between the unin-formed Jeff and the suspected and knowing Rufe for the posses-sion of the pig. The contest is a kind of cornfield stichomythia, gently infused with such Humpty Dumpty words as "casuistically" and "coadjutors", and chock full of comical turns and twists that mark the verbal combat as one of the finest examples of sheer nonsense in the language.[16]

It is "whole hog or none" with Jeff, whose motto, adapted from Wall Street, is "buy low and sell high". Rufe, who has bragged copiously about his deftness in hog-stealing, is dead set to deceive his new partner for the biggest gain in his shoat-purloining career. This clash of personalities carries the narrative along to the de-nouement. To create the "snap", Rufe absconds with his ill-

---

[16]   *The Shorter Oxford Dictionary* defines *stichomythia* thus: In classical Greek Drama, dialogue in alternate lines, employed in sharp disputation, and characterized by antithesis and rhetorical repetition or taking up of the opponent's words. Also applied to modern imitations of this.

gotten gains. At the house where the two have boarded, Mrs. Peevy, the hostess, asks Peters if she should not keep some soup warm for Mr. Tatum till he returns. Jeff replies by saying that if she does she will "more than exhaust for firewood all the coal in the bosom of the earth and all the forests on the outside of it".[17]

Emphasis in "The Ethics of Pig", a story with a distinctive "old Southwestern" flavor, is as much on character as on plot. The portraits of Jefferson Peters, the cheater cheated, and Rufe Tatum, the cheater cheating, are sketched "in little", yet they are done in a hand as sure as that which produced Mercutio.

If O. Henry is a mere entertainer, it is because the chief purpose and aim of a humorist is to "excite the risibilities". Even Shakespeare, when he elected to write in a comic vein, offered playgoers little of the didactic either in speech or in situation. *The Merry Wives of Windsor* would seem to have been written chiefly with the purpose of diverting the audience, and if we are to believe John Dennis, partly to amuse Queen Elizabeth I, the good queen being desirous of seeing the fat knight in love.[18] *The Taming of the Shrew*, to use a current locution, is "good fun", but few, we daresay, would recommend the comedy as a handbook for the wooing of a froward or willful sweetheart. Entertainers as a rule are not a bad lot anyway; much can be said in their defence. It can be set down as a truth worthy to be considered that if most readers were given a choice between an evening with Orm's *Ormulum* or Lucian's *The True History*, the witty Samosatan would win the palm every time.[19]

Besides, we would not want to dismiss O. Henry without indicating at least one instance of direct didacticism in a Southwest story of his. We have in mind "Telemachus Friend". In this story prospective lovers are shown the most effective course to pursue in winning the hand and heart of the fair lady of their choice and intent. It is generally averred that realists of an amorous bent would very likely agree with Telemachus Hicks that

[17] "The Ethics of Pig", *op. cit.*, I, 354.
[18] *The Oxford Companion to English Literature*, p. 54.
[19] *The Works of Lucian of Samosata*, translated by H. W. Fowler and F. G. Fowler. II, 136.

Othello's method of courtship will succeed better on the stage than off.

As for us, we prefer our didacticism in broken doses, indirectly administered; we like the stuff that way, if we like it at all. And if you were to drop by our abode on the sort of day you believed you would more likely find us, the chances are we would be "deep in the interstices" of a diverting story by the ex-druggist of the Columbus prison, or else seeking escape in a piece "in the Greek line", something from Lucian, perhaps, or else a few passages from the blind bard with a deep brow that made Keats feel like stout Cortez when he "stood silent on a peak in Darien".

APPENDIX

BLACK BART

San Francisco, December 4, 1883. The doors of the California State penitentiary at San Quentin have just closed upon one of the most remarkable criminals this country has ever produced, and their name is legion. 'Black Bart, the Po 8', as he styled himself, carries one back to the days of Claude Duval, and, single-handed, he committed more robberies than perhaps any other solitary individual in the annals of crime, for he robbed the stages of the Wells Fargo Express on the Pacific coast twenty-eight times within a few years.

POETICAL AND POLITE

A description of Black Bart's methods, published by the detectives prior to his apprehension, says:

He is generally masked with a flour sack over his face, and an old long linen duster to cover his person. In attacking a stage he usually jumps out in front of the team in a stooping posture and seeks to shield himself in front of the lead horses. He is always armed with a double-barreled shotgun, which he unbreeches, and rolls in his blankets, as soon as he is safe from immediate pursuit; he always brings an old ax to the scene of the robbery, which he uses to open the box, and leaves in the vicinity of the robbery. In opening the mail sacks he cuts them with a sharp knife; thus, T – on top of the sack near the lock. He has never manifested any viciousness, and there is reason to believe that he is averse to taking human life. He is polite to all passengers, and especially so to ladies. He comes and goes from the scene of robbery on foot; seems to be a thorough mountaineer, and a good walker, as he sometimes covers long distances in a day – getting food from houses in out-of-the-way places, but has never been known to remain over night in a house that is occupied; never allows himself to be seen in the vicinity of a robbery, and never shows up for food until twelve or fifteen miles away. His only

visible baggage when travelling is a roll of blankets, generally tied
with bale rope at the ends, although at one time he had a long valise.

Black Bart was a writer of doggerel verse as well as a highwayman. After robbing the stage that runs from Quincy to Croville
on the 25th of July, 1878, he left the following screed in the box:

> Here I lay me down to sleep,
>   To wail the coming morrow;
> Perhaps success, perhaps defeat,
>   And everlasting sorrow.

> I've labored long and hard for bread,
>   For honor and for riches;
> But on my corns too long you've tread,
>   You fine-haired s——s of b——es.

> Let come what will, I'll try it on –
>   My condition can't be worse;
> And if there's money in that box,
>   'Tis money in my purse.
>   Black Bart, the Po. 8.

HIS CAREER AND ITS CLOSE

[The following is from the office of Wells, Fargo & Co., at San
Francisco, and gives additional particulars concerning the career
of Black Bart, and its "wind up".]

For the past eight years, as is now known – that is, since the summer
of 1875 – our express has been repeatedly robbed on the highways
of this state by one man. For a long time our detective officers were
perplexed by his skill and coolness and celerity of movement, but
latterly became satisfied that he made his headquarters in San Francisco; and from glimpses had of the man at various times when
perpetrating robberies, or in the vicinity, a description, which now
proves accurate, was obtained of him, and circulars sent throughout
the country, but without avail. On the 3d of November the stage
was robbed on the Sonora route, and nearly $5000 obtained by the

"lone highwayman," who, being shot at by the driver, and the gold amalgam he had taken weighing eigtheen pounds, was compelled to hurry, and in the excitement of the chase dropped a handkerchief and cuff, which in the subsequent search were found by Sheriff Thorn, of Calaveras county. They having Chinese-laundry marks, led to his early arrest here, and conviction of the robbery, and he is now incarcerated in San Quentin. Since his conviction he has given our officers a succinct list of robberies perpetrated by him alone – numbering twenty-eight (in two of which he was shot by messenger and stage-driver, but escaped) – since the summer of 1875. Here you have a record that would put to blush Claude Duval and Dick Turpin. He is a prepossessing man in appearance, muscularly built, about 5 feet 9 inches high, weighs 165 pounds, and is capable of the most remarkable endurance in walking and mountaineering; is comparatively well educated and a general reader – cool, self-contained, sententious talker, with waggish tendencies; a native of Jefferson county, New York, about forty-eight, but looks fifty-five.

Galveston *Daily News*, December 10, 1883.

"DETECTIVE" PRICE OF TEXAS

This party ['Detective Price'], who has come in for a good share of infamous notoriety with Tennessee's defaulting treasurer, Polk, has an unsavory record, which I have secured from sources of absolute authority. Before the war Price was a special officer of the Police in New Orleans, and was noted for his general crookedness and cussedness. Even at this time he had killed his man, and that in cold blood, standing beside him and in conversation, putting his right hand around his shoulder and shooting him through the head. Price was in the penitentiary when General Butler occupied New Orleans and was liberated by that doughty knight of the spoons. He loafed about New Orleans some time and finally emigrated to Texas about 1869, becoming engaged there as a 'spotter' on the Houston and Texas Central railway, but was discharged for dirty work and drunkenness. For some time after that he lived the life of an adventurer of a low order, and about two years ago attempted to establish a merchants police at Galveston, but finding that Mike Farrell, a celebrated bank detective of New Orleans, intended establishing the same at Galveston, he withdrew from this enterprise and went to San Antonio about six months ago, and immediately flamed out at the head of the "Texas Detective Agency." He has the reputation of not only being a bully, but a coward. A few years ago he gave away some important detective work which was being done by Captain Lee Hall, of the Texas State Police. Hall flatly accused him of his treachery, when Price drew a pistol on the captain. The latter took the revolver from him and pommeled him so unmercifully that he was confined to his room for several weeks.

Another of his infamous pieces of business created quite an excitement some ten years since in New Orleans, when he returned there and was keeping a crooked livery stable. Billy Forrester, probably the most noted bank breaker which ever lived, escaped from the Illinois State penitentiary at Joliet, and being closely followed by the Pinkertons, was arrested under their instruction by Chief of Police Badger of New Orleans. Price, imagining that Forrester had large booty to draw upon, secured the services of Judge Atocha, a quite celebrated criminal lawyer of that day in New Orleans, and effected the release of Forrester on a writ of habeas corpus. Price never got a penny for this, and it almost broke his heart. Forrester was duly recaptured. From all information regarding the man Price, he was a scoundrel and villain; and the police authorities and noted detectives of this city are certain that himself and Cameron must have secured a large sum of money from Polk. As near as can be learned, Cameron, Price's partner, was recently in the service of the government as a special agent of the police department. Louisville *Courier Journal*, as quoted in the Galveston *Daily News*, January 20, 1883.

THE LATE THOMAS W. PEIRCE

Colonel Thomas W. Peirce, president of the Galveston, Harrisburg and San Antonio Railroad company, and a director of the Southern Pacific company, died at Clifton Springs, N.Y., last Friday. Colonel Peirce, though not a Texan either by birth or adoption, was so closely identified with Texas in a commercial and business way that all Texans were more or less interested in his career, achievements and enterprises. Colonel Peirce was in his 68th year at the time of his death. He was born at Dover, N.H., and founded the firm of Peirce & Bacon, merchants and ship owners at Boston in 1840. In 1847 he became largely interested in the Texas trade, and did much to develop the resources of the State and set the wheels of progress in motion. He was one of the first of the conservative business men of the North to see the great possibilities of Texas, and as soon as he made the discovery he made his plans to capture the Texas trade. Colonel Peirce was a progressive, enterprising and public-spirited business man, and not a professional philanthropist. Every move he made was in his own interest. It must be said, however, that his enterprises were beneficial to the public and generally met with the public approval. He first came to Texas, in 1842, landing at Galveston, and he went as far west as San Antonio. During this trip the idea of the Galveston, Harrisburg and San Antonio railroad first occurred to him, and afterward, when General Sidney Sherman attempted to put the idea in execution, he had the warm support of Colonel Peirce. Not until after the war, however, did Colonel Peirce interest himself in Texas railroad enterprises. From 1847 until the breaking out of the war he maintained a fleet of twelve or fourteen ships plying between Boston, Galveston and Liverpool. He engaged largely in the cotton trade, but the civil war killed his business in that line, and he severed his connection with Texas until the cessation of hostilities. After the war he turned his attention to railroad development. His only previous connection with Texas railroads was as the commission merchant who purchased the first iron for the old Houston and Texas Central track. His connection with the Galveston, Houston and Henderson railroad, with subsequent complications, need not be recounted. After this connection he engaged in the development of the Sunset road, with which he maintained a connection active or nominal until the time of his death. The telegraph dispatches state that Colonel Peirce was worth some $10,000,000 at the time of his death. This is doubtful; in fact those best acquainted with his affairs here are inclined to think that when his interests and obligations are cast up, there will not be much on either side of the ledger.

Galveston *Daily News*, October 4, 1885.

A MILLIONAIRE'S WILL

The Will of the Late Thos. W. Peirce Filed for Record.

Everybody in Texas knew the late Thos. W. Peirce, who died several years ago at Dover, Mass. He was practically the builder of the Galveston, Harrisburg and San Antonio railroad – the Sunset route – now a part and parcel of the Southern Pacific system.

Mr. Peirce died possessed of several million dollars. After providing liberally for children and their issue, leaving them an immense lot of landed estate and $2,250,000 in cash, he bequeaths about $1,000,000 to other relatives ranging in various amounts from $1000 to $100,000. To his brother, Andrew Peirce, he leaves $100,000 and to his nephew, Thos. W. Peirce, $100,000. To Mr. and Mrs. R. S. Spofford he bequeaths $75,000. To his friends, Chas. Babbidge of Boston $25,000; Jas. Converse of Houston, $10,000 and C. C. Gibbs, $5000.

He directs that his trustees shall have prepared souvenirs of the value of $500 each, to be presented to the following named persons as a testimonial of the friendship borne them by the deceased: Hon. Jeremiah Black of New York, Hon. John H. George of Concord, N.H., Hon. Josiah G. Abbott of Massachusetts, Hon. Levi Woodbury of Boston, Hon. Benjamin F. Butler of Massachusetts and Mr. Collis P. Huntington of New York.

The will contains a number of charitable bequests, among them $20,000 for a charity hospital, to be located along the line of the Galveston, Harrisburg and San Antonio road, between Houston and San Antonio, for the care of employes who may be injured on that road; $20,000 for a memorial church at Dover, Mass.; $10,000 for a religious society at Dover; $500 a year for the maintenance of a popular lecture course at Topsfield, Mass.; $500 a year to the Consumptives' home in Mass., and to the towns of Schulenberg, Flatonia, Marion, Luling, Waelder, Weimar and Columbus, on the line of the Galveston, Harrisburg and San Antonio road, he bequeathed $2000 each for the cause of public education and $1000 each to the towns of Ellinger and Harwood for the same purpose.

Galveston *Daily News*, February 2, 1890.

BIBLIOGRAPHY

Life and Adventures of Sam Bass (Dallas, 1878).

Giovanni Boccaccio, *The Decameron* (London, no date).

Herbert Eugene Bolton, *Athanase de Mézières and the Louisiana-Texas Frontier, 1768-1780* (Cleveland, 1914).

Julius Cahn, *Theatrical Guide*, Vol. III (New York, 1898).

Bartley Campbell, "The White Slave and Other Plays", *America's Lost Plays*, XIX, ed. Napier Wilt (Bloomington, 1965).

Lewis Carroll, *Alice in Wonderland* and *Through the Looking Glass* (New York, 1945).

Frederick C. Chabot, *With the Makers of San Antonio* (San Antonio, 1937).

James Fenimore Cooper, *The Prairie* (New York and Toronto, 1950).

William Corner, *San Antonio de Bexar, a Guide and History* (San Antonio, 1890).

Joseph Francis Daly, *The Life of Augustin Daly* (New York, 1917).

Charles Dance, *Naval Engagements* (London, 1838).

Robert H. Davis and Arthur B. Maurice, *The Caliph of Bagdad* (New York and London, 1931).

Charles Dickens, *Works, Crown edition* (London, 1896).

J. Frank Dobie, *A Vaquero of the Brush Country* (Dallas, 1929).

C. Douglas, *Famous Texas Feuds* (Dallas, 1936).

Sir Arthur Conan Doyle, *The Complete Sherlock Holmes Short Stories* (London, 1928).

Edward Eggleston, *The Hoosier Schoolmaster* (New York, 1957).

Chris Emmett, *Shanghai Pierce, A Fair Likeness* (Norman, 1953).

Joseph S. Gallegly, *Footlights on the Border* (The Hague, 1962).

Charles Mills Gayley, *The Classic Myths in English Literature and in Art* (Boston, 1911).

Katherine Goodale, *Behind the Scenes with Edwin Booth* (Boston and New York, 1931).

Edwina Booth Grossman, *Recollections of Edwin Booth* (New York, 1902).

John Wesley Hardin, *The Life of John Wesley Hardin, As Written by Himself* (Seguin, 1895).

G. W. Harris, *Sut Lovingood* (New York, 1867).

Bret Harte, *The Writings of Bret Harte* (Boston and New York, 1896-1906).

O. Henry, *The Complete Works of O. Henry*, two volumes (New York, 1953).

Johnson Jones Hooper, *Simon Sugg's Adventures* (Philadelphia, 1881).
Charles Hoyt, "Five Plays", *America's Lost Plays*, IX, ed. Douglas Hunt (Bloomington, 1964).
Laurence Hutton, *Plays and Players* (New York, 1875).
Al Jennings, *Through the Shadows with O. Henry* (New York, 1921).
N. A. Jennings, *A Texas Ranger* (Dallas, 1930).
Virgil Carrington Jones, *The Hatfields and the McCoys* (Chapel Hill, 1948).
August Frederic Ferdinand von Kotzebue, "The Stranger", *French's Standard Drama*, No. IX, ed. Epes Sargent (New York, no date).
Gerald Langford, *Alias O. Henry* (New York, 1957).
Lillie Langtry, *The Days I Knew* (New York, 1925).
Tom Lea, *The Brave Bulls* (Boston, 1949).
E. Hudson Long, *O. Henry, The Man and His Work* (Philadelphia, 1949).
A. B. Longstreet, *Georgia Scenes* (New York, 1957).
Sadie E. Martin, *Life and Professional Career of Emma Abbott* (Minneapolis, 1891).
Munsey's Magazine, XXVIII, No. 1 (October, 1902).
Henry D. and Frances T. McCallum, *The Wire That Fenced the West* (Norman, 1966).
McClure's Magazine, XXV, XXVI, XXX (1905).
The New York Drama, A Choice Collection of Tragedies, Comedies, Farces, Etc., III, IV (New York, 1876, 1878).
Allardyce Nicoll, *A History of English Drama*, IV, second edition (Cambridge, 1955).
George C. D. Odell, *Annals of the New York Stage*, 15 vols. (New York 1927-1949).
Oxford Companion to American Literature, ed. James D. Hart (New York, 1948).
Oxford Companion to English Literature, second edition, ed. Sir Paul Harvey (Oxford, 1937).
Arthur W. Page, "Little Pictures of O. Henry", *The Complete Works of O. Henry*, one vol. (New York, 1928).
Fred Lewis Pattee, *Mark Twain* (New York and Cincinnati, 1935).
H. P. Phelps, *Players of a Century*, 2nd ed. (Albany, 1880).
Edgar Allan Poe, "The Fall of the House of Usher", *The Complete Works of Edgar Allan Poe*, ed. James A. Harrison (New York, 1902).
Arthur Hobson Quinn, *A History of American Drama, from the Civil War to the Present Day* (New York, 1927).
François Rabelais, *Gargantua and Pantagruel* (London, 1929).
Dora Neil Raymond, *Captain Lee Hall of Texas* (Norman, 1940).
Edwin Le Roy Rice, *Monarchs of Minstrelsy* (New York, 1911).
Bruce Roberts, *Springs From the Parched Ground* (Uvalde, 1950).
San Antonio *City Directory, 1883-1884*.
George Santayana, *Dominations and Powers* (New York, 1957).
William Shakespeare, *The Works of Shakespeare*, 7 vols., ed. Lewis Theobald (London, 1733).
The Shorter Oxford Dictionary, 3rd edition, revised with addenda (Oxford, 1959).
Charles A. Siringo, *Riata and Spurs* (Boston and New York, 1931).

C. Alphonso Smith, *O. Henry Biography* (Garden City and New York, 1916).

Southwestern Historical Quarterly, LXI, No. 2 (October, 1957).

Lewis G. Strang, *Famous Actors of the Day in America* (Boston, 1900).

Alex E. Sweet and J. Armory Knox, *On a Mexican Mustang Through Texas* (Hartford, 1883).

N. A. Taylor, *Coming Empire, or Two Thousand Miles in Texas on Horseback* (New York, Boston and New Orleans, 1877).

Frank X. Tolbert, *An Informal History of Texas*, 1st edition (New York, 1961).

Leo Tolstoy, *War and Peace*, trans. Constance Garnett (New York, no date).

The Trail Drivers of Texas, compiled by J. Marvin Hunter (San Antonio, 1920).

Ben C. Truman, *The Field of Honor* (New York, 1884).

Mark Twain, *The Writings of Mark Twain*, Author's National Edition (New York and London, 1911).

Wm. W. Walton, *Life and Adventures of Ben Thompson, the Famous Texan* (Austin, 1884).

Frederick Warde, *Fifty Years of Make Believe* (New York, 1920).

W. P. Webb, *The Texas Rangers* (Boston and New York, 1925).

Newspapers

The *Evening Paper*
The Galveston *Daily News*
The Houston *Daily Post*
The Houston *Weekly Telegraph*
The New Orleans *Times-Democrat*
The San Antonio *Daily Express*
The San Antonio *Evening Light*
The *Surprise*

INDEX

STUDIES IN AMERICAN LITERATURE

17. GEORGE BRANDON SAUL: *Quintet: Essays on Five American Women Poets*. 1967. 50 pp. ƒ 10.—

19. PHYLLIS FRANKLIN: *Show Thyself a Man: A Comparison of Benjamin Franklin and Cotton Mather*. 1969. 93 pp. ƒ 21.—

22. JONAS SPATZ: *Hollywood in Fiction: Some versions of the American Myth*. 1969. 148 pp. ƒ 28.—

23. STEPHEN A. BLACK: *James Thurber. His Masquerades: A Critical Study*. 1969. 128 pp. ƒ 24.—

26. C. A. M. JANSSENS: *The American Literary Review: A Critical History, 1920-1950*. 1968. 341 pp. ƒ 38.—

MOUTON · PUBLISHERS · THE HAGUE